Ṛṣikās
of the Ṛgveda

Ṛṣikās of the Ṛgveda

Swamini Atmaprajnananda Saraswati

DK PRINTWORLD
Publishers of Indian Traditions

Cataloging in Publication Data — DK
[Courtesy: D.K. Agencies (P) Ltd. <docinfo@dkagencies.com>]

Atmaprajnananda Saraswati, Swamini, 1955-
Ṛsikās of the Ṛgveda / Swamini Atmaprajnananda Saraswati.
p. cm.
In Sanskrit; translation and introductory matter in English.
Includes bibliographical references (p.).
ISBN 13: 9788124606568

1. Rishis in the Vedas. 2. Women in literature. 3. Vedas. Ṛgveda — Criticism, interpretation, etc. I. Vedas. Ṛgveda. English & Sanskrit. Selections II. Title.

DDC 294.5921046 23

ISBN 13: 978-81-246-0656-8 ISBN 10: 81-246-0656-0
First published in India in 2013

Printed and published by:
D.K. Printworld (P) Ltd.
Regd. Office : *'Vedaśrī'*, F-395, Sudarshan Park
(Metro Station: Ramesh Nagar)
New Delhi - 110 015
Phones : (011) 2545 3975; 2546 6019; *Fax* : (011) 2546 5926
e-mail : indology@dkprintworld.com
Web : www.dkprintworld.com

to all those women of the past and present,
noted or forgotten,

who brought pride to
the female fraternity,

who constitute half the human population of this planet,

who can think, reflect, have their independent opinion,
and work through their limbs,

who indulged deeply
to sustain the family, the community,
the society, the nation, the world, sans revolt,

those who spoke, and those who remained silent,

to all those, who showed their strength,

so that I could discover mine.

Preface

LIKE *Ulysses*[1] of James Joyce, *Ṛṣikās of the Ṛgveda* was a single page in my book *Nomenclature of the Vedas*. It became fifty-one pages by September 2010 and then blossomed into 151 pages now.

I want this book to reach all the women — achievers in diverse fields of activity — spiritual-cum-religious leaders, research scholars, educationists, physicians, lawyers, judges, administrators, social activists, business tycoons, classical dancers, singers, painters, literary figures, film makers, sports persons, astronauts, scientists, designers, media personalities and all those young women who are dreaming big. Some contend that many of the listed *ṛṣikās* are concepts without a face or form. Fine, even if there is just one Kalpana Chawla or Sunita Williams among the multitude of women, the statement is made.

Since the free translation[2] is provided, I come under the blue sky and am vulnerable. Readers are not to blame me about the contents of the hymns.

---

1. The idea grew from a story in *Dubliners* in 1906, to a short book in 1907, to a vast novel that James Joyce began in 1914.
2. The translations are based on R.T.H. Griffith's *The Hymns of the Ṛgveda*; A.A. Macdonell's *A Vedic Reader for Students*; and Hanns-Peter Schmidt's *Apālā-Sūkta*. I have substituted the Victorian English pronominal forms with corresponding terms in modern English for better understanding. I have also replaced some archaic words whose meanings have changed over a century.

Sāyaṇa quoted the *Bhāgavatam* in his *Taittirīya-Saṁhitā-Bhāṣya-Bhūmikā* in the fourteenth century:

strīśūdra-dvijabandhūnāṁ trayī na śrutigocarā ।
karmaśreyasi mūḍhānāṁ śreya eva bhaved-iha ।
iti bhāratam-ākhyānaṁ muninā kṛpayā kṛtam ॥
— *Bhāgavatam,* I.4.25

It only shows that a great scholar may not sometimes be so empathetic. In Reiki's language it is explained, "the person's *ājñā cakra* has opened up, but *anāhata cakra* (heart-*cakra*) has not opened up". This is seconded by the fact that his elder brother, Mādhavācārya justified[3] the practice of *satī*.

The actual import of *upanayanam* is to lead the child to the teacher for Vedic studies. In course of time, this essential practice became a mere ritual — a thread-ceremony. *Upanayanam* ceremonies were no more being held for the females, because in course of time, child-marriage became the convention, so that the girl-child's fertility period is not wasted. The cognitive deprivation gradually brought down the social status of the women at par with the śūdras. It is rather amazing that the bards at the time of compilation of the *Ṛgveda* did not delete *Yama-Yamī-Saṁvāda*, much less the other Vedic hymns partially, collectively or alternatively seen or envisioned by the females.

My contention is: only the Veda, that is given the status of *apauruṣeya,* has to state that it is not available or should be out of reach to the females, and not a historical *pauruṣeya*-text, i.e. any Dharmaśāstra, much less a Purāṇa.

It is of great significance to note that Yājñavalkya did not refuse to answer Gārgī's spirited questions, and that in his huge *gurukulam,* where all the four Vedas were being taught

3. Wikipedia — Sati (Practice).

by him,[4] he found Maitreyī to be an *uttama adhikārī* to impart *brahma-vidyā*. No gender bias!

Enough of discussion on the sympathetic and broad-minded *ācārya*s of the past. In our own tradition of Ārṣa-Vidyā, my spiritual Guru Swami Dayananda Saraswati (b. 1930) has made the Vedic/Vedāntic learning freely available to *adhikārī*s that include many females. I boasted with a former diplomat, a newcomer to our *gurukulam*, "Swami Chinmayanadaji brought about a revolution in the 1950s by making the Vedic/Vedāntic teachings available to us. It is because of him that today we women are being able to chant *Rudram* and *Oṁ*," she shot back, "What are you talking! It was long before that, 150 years ago Swami Dayananda Saraswati (CE 1824-83), founder of the Arya Samaj, popularized the Vedic teachings, and we women were encouraged to study the Vedas and perform Vedic *havan*s everyday." Her response enlightened and humbled me.

In our Ārṣa-Vidya tradition, we now have more than 80 female *sannyāsini*s (Hindu nuns) against a total 212 Sannyasis. One of my Ācāryās, Swamini Brahmaprakashananda Saraswati has taught successfully two 3-year Residential Courses on Vedānta, Pāṇini, to around twenty students in our Nagpur Gurukulam. The Ācāryās who taught us Vedic chanting were two senior *Sannyāsinis*. They lead the Vedic chants daily in the Śrī Medhā Dakṣiṇāmūrti Temple at AVG, Anaikatti, which is a traditional temple that observes all the rules of the Āgama Śāstra.

Responding to many hidden and disguised camouflaged questions at various *satsaṅga*s, my Guru, Pujya Swami Dayananda Saraswati, who himself is a living *ṛṣi* and a great authority on interpretation of the Vedas, has clarified thus:

4. See *Śāṅkarabhāṣyam* on *Bṛ. Up*., III.1.2.

> *sādhana-catuṣṭaya* that includes *śamādi-ṣaṭka-sampatti* is the only qualification. The Śāstra (Vedānta) does not specify anything else.

I suggest two books[5] to be read by all those readers who wish to know how the women for centuries together were deprived of the Vedic learning, or for that matter, any other kind of education.

Makara Saṅkrānti,
Uttarāyaṇa
15 January 2012

Atmaprajnananda Saraswati

5. A.S. Altekar, *The Position of Women in Hindu Civilisation, from Prehistoric Times to the Present Day*, Delhi: Motilal Banarsidass; Rajbali Pandey, *Hindu Saṁskāras: Socio-Religious Study of the Hindu Sacraments*, Delhi: Motilal Banarsidass.

Contents

Preface vii

Acknowledgement xiii

Abbreviations xiv

Notes on Transliteration xv

Women Ṛṣis (Ṛṣikās) in the Ṛgveda 1

PART I

Who Praised the Deities

1. Ghoṣā Kākṣīvatī 6
2. Godhā 16
3. Viśvavārā Ātreyī 19
4. Apālā Ātreyī 22
5. Juhū-Brahmajāyā 25
6. Agastya-svasā 28
7. Aditi-Dākṣāyaṇī 32

PART II

Who Conversed with the Seers and Deities

8. Indrāṇī 40
9. Indramātaraḥ 49
10. Saramā Devaśuni 51
11. Romaśā 55
12. Urvaśī 58
13. Lopāmudrā 64
14. Nadyaḥ — The Rivers 67

15. Yamī Vaivasvatī 72
16. Śaśvatī Āṅgirasī 78

PART III

Who Praised the Self

17. Sārparājñī 88
18. Vāgāmbhṛṇī 90
19. Śraddhā Kāmāyanī 93
20. Dakṣiṇā Prājāpatyā 95
21. Rātri-Bhāradvājī 99
22. Sūryā-Sāvitrī 102

PART IV

Other Ṛṣikās not Listed in Bṛhaddevatā

23. Śacī Paulomī 118
24. Śikhaṇḍinī Kāśyapī 121
25. Indrasnuṣā-Vasukrapatnī 123

Appendices

A. Ṛṣikās of the Yajurveda 127
Lopāmudrā, Saraśvatī, Kaśipā Bharadvājaduhitā, Viśvavārā Ātreyī, Sārparājñī
B. Ṛṣikās of the Sāmaveda 129
Godhā, Indramātaraḥ, Sārparājñī
C. Ṛṣikās of the Atharvaveda 130
Indrāṇī, Indramātaraḥ, Sūryā-Sāvitrī, Sārparājñī
D. Gārgī Vācaknavī 131
E. Maitreyī 132
Conclusion 133
Glossary 137
Bibliography 147
Index 149

Acknowledgement

MY grateful thanks to,

- Dr. Martha Doherty, for offering enormous encouragement and appreciation for the effort, and inspiring me to incorporate the original *sūkta*s and their free English translations.
- Shri Sanjay Rout for providing the diacritical software,
- Shri Bibhuti Mohapatra, for painstakingly having the *sūkta*s incorporated in Devanāgarī, and English within the deadline.
- Shri Akshay Kumar for immediately providing a new laptop in September 2009, when both my laptops crashed one after the other within fifteen days, erasing all my work of ten years,
- Smt. Payal Parija, for her consistent support during my years of studies and research,
- All the Vedic scholars and researchers, on whose vast work, this tiny attempt stands.

My special gratitude to Shri Susheel Kumar Mittal, Director, D.K. Printworld, for accepting the manuscript and agreeing to publish it. As per our scriptures, every one has five debts to repay during one's lifetime – *Deva-r̥ṇam, R̥ṣi-r̥ṇam, Pitr̥-r̥ṇam, Nr̥-r̥ṇam,* and *Bhūta-r̥ṇam*. By publishing the manuscript, he has helped me in repaying *R̥ṣi-r̥ṇam*.

My surrender to Vedamātā and Devī Saraswatī (They are not different from each other).

Uttarāyaṇa, Makara Saṅkrānti **Atmaprajnananda Saraswati**
15 January 2012

Abbreviations

Ai.Br.	*Aitareya Brāhmaṇa*
Anu.Bhā	*Anu.Bhāṣyam*
AV	*Atharvaveda*
R̥V	*R̥gveda*
R̥V.Sā.Bh.	*R̥gveda-Sāyaṇa-Bhāṣya*
R̥VS	*R̥gveda-Saṁhitā*
Go.Br.	*Gopatha Brāhmaṇa*
Ja.Br.	*Jaiminīya Brāhmaṇa*
Tai.Ār.	*Taittirīya Āraṇyaka*
Tai.Saṁ.	*Taittirīya-Saṁhitā*
Br̥.Up	*Br̥hadāraṇyaka-Upaniṣad*
Br̥had.	*Br̥haddevatā*
Ma.Nā.Up.	*Mahānārayaṇa Upaniṣad*
Ma.Bhā.	*Mahābhārata*
Śa.Br.	*Śatapatha Brāhmaṇa*
ŚYV.Ma.Bh.	*Yajurveda Mahīdhara-Bhāṣya*
Sar.	*Sarvānukramaṇī*
SV	*Sāmaveda*
Ve.Sā.	*Vedāntasāra*
YV	*Yajurveda*

Note on Transliteration

IN this book, Devanāgarī characters are transliterated according to the scheme adopted by the International Congress of Orientalists at Athens in 1912, and since then generally acknowledged to be the only rational and satisfactory one. In it, the inconsistency, irregularity and redundancy of English spelling are ruled out. The letters f, q, w, x and z are not called to use. One fixed value is given to each letter. Hence, a, e, i and g always represent अ, ए, इ, and ग respectively, and never ए, इ, ऐ and ज् or other values which they have in English. The letters t and d are always used for त् and द् only. One tialde (˜), one accent, four macrons (ˉ) and ten dots (2 above, 8 below) are used to represent adequately and correctly all Sanskrit letters. The letter c alone represents च्. Since the natural function of h will be to make the aghoṣa into ghoṣa (e.g. kh, ch, ṭh, th, ph, gh, jh, ḍh, dh, bh), it would be an anomaly for a scientific scheme to use it in combinations like ch and sh for giving च् and ष् values; hence ch here is छ् and sh स् ह्. The vowel ऋ is represented by r̥ because ri is legitimate for रि only, and the singular ri is an altogether objectionable distortion. The tialde (˜) over n represents ञ्, ñ. Accent mark over s gives श्, ś; dots above m and n give anusvāra. (ं), ṁ and ङ्, ṅ, respectively. Dot below h gives visarga (:) ḥ, and a round below r represents ऋ, r̥. Dots below s, n, t and d give their corresponding cerebrals ष्, ण्, ट्, and ड्, ṣ, ṇ, ṭ and ḍ; and macrons (ˉ) over a, i, u and r̥ give आ, ई, ऊ, and ॠ ā, ī, ū, r̥̄ respectively. Macrons (ˉ) are not used to lengthen the quantity of e and o, because they always have the long quantity in Sanskrit. Sanskrit words are capitalised only where special distinctiveness is called for, as in the opening of a sentence, title of books, etc. The scheme of transliteration in full is as follows:

अ a,	आ ā,
इ i,	ई ī,
उ u,	ऊ ū,
ऋ ṛ,	ॠ ṝ,
ए e,	ओ o,
ऐ ai,	औ ou,
ं ṁ,	: ḥ,
क् k,	ख् kh,
ग् g,	घ् gh,
ङ् ṅ,	च् c,
छ् ch,	ज् j,
झ् jh,	ञ् ñ,
ट् ṭ,	ठ् ṭh,
ड् ḍ,	ढ् ḍh,
ण् ṇ,	त् t,
थ् th,	द् d,
ध् dh,	न् n,
प् p,	फ् ph,
ब् b,	भ् bh,
म् m,	य् y,
र् r,	ल् l,
व् v,	श् ś,
ष् ṣ,	स् s,
ह् h.	

Women Ṛṣis (Ṛṣikās) in the Ṛgveda

IN the *Ṛgveda* the persons who had special experiences are called the Ṛṣis. Throughout the ages the Ṛṣis have been held as the objects of the highest reverence. The Vedic *mantra*s, in fact, are the records of the spiritual realisations and experiences of the Ṛṣis. The Ṛṣis experienced the truth, had the revelations, or ability to receive hearing messages of the truth. They are also called seers (*mantra-draṣṭāraḥ*) because they literally could observe the actions of the cosmic powers. A Ṛṣi was a person (male or female) of deep contemplation. S/he was perhaps not necessarily a scholar or an intellectual, but s/he had access to intuition, inspiration and other superior modes of exposure to knowledge and action.

A verse of *Ṛgveda* is called a *ṛk* or the word of illumination. A Ṛṣi is one who has a vision of the *ṛk* or a supra-physical state of hearing of the *ṛk*. All the *mantra*s of *ṚVS* put together have been revealed to around 400 Ṛṣis, of whom at least 27 were women, such as Vāgāṁbhṛṇi (seer of *ṚV* X.125) Sūryā-Sāvitrī (*ṚV* X.85), Ghoṣā Kākṣīvatī (*ṚV* X.39 and *ṚV* X.40), Aditi-Dākṣāyaṇī (*ṚV* X.72), Apālā Ātreyī (*ṚV* VIII.91), Dakṣiṇā Prājāpatyā (*ṚV* X.107), etc.

Each verse of *ṚVS* is a complete *mantra*. A Ṛṣi in the *ṚV* is a person who has had the revelation of at least one *ṛk* of the *ṚV*. The Ṛṣi literally hears the *mantra* by supra-physical methods. Sometimes the Ṛṣi receives the inspiration, and s/he may supply appropriate words and the metre to complete it. Since the Ṛṣi has supra-physical visions of the Truth, s/he is also called a seer (*draṣṭā*).

It may be noted that no one is born as a Ṛṣi. Being a son or daughter of a Ṛṣi does not automatically confer on the person the powers of the Ṛṣi, although there are sons and daughters of *ṛṣi*s, who are also Ṛṣis/Ṛṣikās. Some such examples are — Apālā Ātreyī, daughter of Ṛṣi Atri, Śāśvatī Āṅgirasī, daughter of Ṛṣi Aṅgiras, Śikhaṇḍinī Kāśyapī, the two daughters of Ṛṣi Kaśyapa. A person performs special spiritual practices, including *tapas,* to become a Ṛṣi. There is no specific procedure for becoming a Ṛṣi. One can only become a Ṛṣi by the grace of the cosmic powers or the *devatā*s. We have the example of Ṛṣikā Ghoṣā Kākṣīvatī who was blessed by the Aśvins with two *sūkta*s in the *Ṛgveda* (X.39 and X.40), each of them of 14 *mantra*s. In *ṚV* I.31.16 Agni is said to create or form a Ṛṣi (*ṛṣikṛt*). Similarly, *ṚV* IX.96.18 declares that Soma creates seers.

A Ṛṣi is identified by two names, his/her own name, and that of his/her father or the lineage (*gotra*). The first *sūkta* of *ṚVS* was revealed to Madhucchandāḥ Vaiśvāmitraḥ, a son or disciple of Viśvāmitra. The famous *Gāyatrī-mantra* *ṚV* III.62.10 was revealed to Viśvāmitra Gāthina, i.e. Viśvāmitra, the son of Gāthin. The daughter of Ṛṣi Kakṣivān is Ghoṣā Kākṣīvatī, who is the *ṛṣikā* of *ṚV* X.39 and X.40. Ṛṣikā Apālā Ātreyī is the daughter of Ṛṣi Ātreya. Ṛṣikā Yamī Vaivasvatī is the daughter of Vivasvān. Ṛṣikā Śaśvatī Āṅgirasī is the daughter of Ṛṣi Aṅgiras. Ṛṣikā Dakṣiṇā Prājāpatyā is the daughter of Prajāpati. Ṛṣikās Śikhaṇḍinī Kāśyapī are the two daughters of Ṛṣi Kaśyapa. Ṛṣikā Śacī Paulomī is the daughter of the demon king Puloma. The name of the Ṛṣi/Ṛṣikā indicates the gender clearly.

In the Vedic literature, great respect is offered to the Seers. Equal importance is given to the women Ṛṣikās irrespective of their gender. Women of the Vedic period (around 4500-2500 BCE) were epitomes of spiritual attainments. The Vedas have volumes to say about these spiritual women. The gender discrimination is a later phenomenon. Gradually, a general opinion was formed that women are not *adhikārī*s for the study of the Vedas. However such an injunction is nowhere available in the Vedas. Many non-Vedic as well as Vedic scholars may not be knowing that there are at least twenty-seven women *mantra-draṣṭāraḥ* in the *Ṛgveda*. Being able to receive and decipher a *mantra* has nothing to do with somebody's gender. In this thesis, a comprehensive list of women Ṛṣikās, their brief introduction, the *mantra*s seen to them, as well as the subject matter of the *mantra*s is being provided for the benefit of the readers.

Who is a Ṛṣi? As per the definition, *yasya vākyaṁ sa ṛṣi*. Bṛhaddevatākāra Ṛṣi Śaunaka has presented twenty-seven Ṛṣikās in three *śloka*s in *Bṛhaddevatā*.

ghoṣā godhā viśvavārā apālopaniṣanniṣat ।
brahmajāyā juhūrnāma agastyasya svasāditi ।। II.82.
indrāṇī cendramātā ca saramā romaśorvaśī ।
lopāmudrā ca nadyaśca yamī nārī ca śaśvatī ।। II.83.
śrīrlākṣā sārparājñī vāk śraddhā medhā ca dakṣiṇā ।
rātrī sūryā ca sāvitrī brahmavādinya iritāḥ ।। II.84

Ghoṣā, Godhā, Viśvavārā, Apālā, Upaniṣad, Niṣad, Brahmajāyā (who is) named Juhū, Agastya-svāsā (the sister of Agastya), Aditi. (82) And Indrāṇī, and the mother of Indra, Saramā, Romaśā, Urvaśī, and Lopāmudrā, and the Rivers, (and) Yamī and the wife Śaśvatī. (83) Śrī, Lākṣā, Sārparājñī, Vāk, Śraddhā,

Medhā, Dakṣiṇā, Rātrī, and Sūryā Sāvitrī, (all these) are pronounced to be female seers. (84).

navakaḥ prathamastvāsām vargastuṣṭāva devatāḥ ।
ṛṣibhir-devatābhiśca samūde madhyamo gaṇaḥ ।। II. 85.
ātmano bhāvavṛttāni jagau vargas-tathottamaḥ ।
uttamasya tu vargasya ya ṛṣiḥ saiva devatā ।। II.86.
ātmānam-astaud-vargastu devatāṁ yas-tathottamaḥ ।
tasmād-ātmastaveṣu syād ya ṛṣiḥ, saiva devatā ।। II.87.

The first group of these, consisting of nine, praised the deities; the middle series conversed with seers and deities (85). The last group sang the evolutionary forms (*bhāvavṛttam*) of the Self. So, whoever is the seer (of a hymn by one) of the last group, is also the deity (86). Each Seer of the last group thus praised herself as the deity: therefore, whosoever may be the seer in self-laudations, is at the same time the deity (87)[1].

1. *Bṛhad.*, tr. A.A. Macdonell, p. 56.

Part I
Who Praised the Deities

1

Ghoṣā Kākṣīvatī

VEDIC wisdom is encapsulated in myriads of hymns, and twenty-seven women seers emerge from there itself. However, most of them are abstractions except for a few, such as Ghoṣā, who has a definite human form. She is the seer of two *sūkta*s in the *Ṛgveda* (X.39 containing fourteen *mantra*s, eulogising the Aśvins, the heavenly physician twins; and X.40, also containing fourteen *mantra*s, is a personal wish expressing her own intimate feelings and desires of a married life).

She was a princess, daughter of Ṛṣi Kakṣivān, hence the adjective Kākṣīvatī, and the granddaughter of Ṛṣi Dīrghatamas, both composers of hymns in praise of the Aśvins. There is a reference in *ṚV* I.117.7 seen by Ṛṣi Kakṣivān Dairghatamā stating that she obtained her husband because of the grace of the Aśvin Kumārs. *Bṛhaddevatā* has her life story as thus, — Ghoṣā, daughter of Kakṣivān, was disfigured by an incurable disease, probably leprosy, and remained unmarried at her father's house for sixty years. She fell into great grief (thinking),

> 'Without son or husband I have reached old age in vain; I (will) therefore resort to the Lord of Light (Śubhaspati). Since my father (Ṛṣi Kakṣivān Dairghatamā) by propitiating them, obtained his youth, long life, health, power, poison for slaying all beings, I, his daughter, (would obtain) beauty and good fortune, and if to me are also revealed *mantra*s, in those the Aśvins shall be praised by me.'

As she reflected thus, she saw the two *sūktas*: *yo vāṁ parijmā suvṛdaśvinā* and *rathaṁ yāntaṁ kuha*. Her implorations with the celestial Aśvins, and the devotion of her ancestors towards them made them cure her disease, and allow her to experience the wedding bliss. They made her ageless, free from disease, and beautiful (*subhaga*). They gave her a husband, and a son who subsequently became a sage (Suhastya). Incidentally, her son Sage Suhastya Ghauṣeya[1] is the seer of the next *sūkta*, *ṚV* X.41, also addressed to the Aśvins. Ācārya Sāyaṇa has presented her as the worthy daughter of Kakṣivān — *kakṣivato duhitā nāma brahmavādinyarṣiḥ*.[2]

ṚV X.39
(14 mantras)

ऋषि – काक्षीवती। देवता – अश्विनौ।
छन्द – जगती, १४ त्रिष्टुप्।

Ṛṣikā — Ghoṣā Kākṣīvatī; Devatā — Aśvins
Metre — Jagatī, 14-Triṣṭup

यो वां परिज्मा सुवृदश्विना रथो दोषामुषासो हव्यो हविष्मता।
शश्वत्तमासस्तमु वामिदं वयं पितुर्न नाम सुहवं हवामहे।।१।।

As'twere the name of father, easy to invoke,
We all assembled here to invoke this Car of yours,
Aśvins! Your swift-rolling circumambient Car,
Which he who worships,
Must invoke at eve and dawn.

चोदयतं सूनृताः पिन्वतं धिय उत् पुरंधीरीरयतं तदुश्मसि।
यशसं भागं कृणुतं नो अश्विना सोमं न चारुं मघवत्सु नस्कृतम्।।२।।

1. Like Kaunteya, Suhastya's second name is after his mother Ghoṣā.
2. *ṚV.Sā.Bh.*, X.39.

Awake all pleasant strains,
And let the hymns flow forth,
Raise up abundant fullness, this is our desire.
Aśvins! Bestow on us a glorious heritage,
And give our princes treasure fair as Soma is.

अमाजुरश्चिद्भवथो युवं भगोऽनाशोश्चिदवितारापमस्य चित्।
अन्धस्य चिन्नासत्या कृशस्य चिद्युवामिदाहुर्भिषजा रुतस्य चित्।।३।।

You are the bliss of her, who grows old at home,
And helpers of the slow although he linger last.
Men call you too, Nāsatyas! Healers of the blind,
The thin and feeble, and the man with broken bones.

युवं च्यवानं सनयं यथा रथं पुनर्युवानं च रथाय तक्षथुः।
निष्टौग्र्यमूहथुरद्भ्यस्परि विश्वेत्ता वां सवनेषु प्रवाच्या।।४।।

You made Cyavāna, weak and worn with
length of days, young again like a car,
That he had power to move.
You lifted up the son of Tugra from the floods.
At our libations must all these your acts be praised.

पुराणा वां वीर्या३ प्र ब्रवा जनेऽथो हासथुर्भिषजा मयोभुवा।
तां वां नु नव्याववसे करामहेऽयं नासत्या श्रदुरिर्यथा दधत्।।५।।

We will declare among the folk,
Your ancient deeds heroic,
Yes, you were Physicians bringing health.
You, you who must be lauded,
Will we bring for aid, so that this foe of ours,
O Aśvins! May believe.

इयं वामह्वे शृणुतं मे अश्विना पुत्रायेव पितरा मह्यं शिक्षतम्।
अनापिरज्ञा असजात्यामतिः पुरा तस्या अभिशस्तेरव स्पृतम्।।६।।

Listen to me, O Aśvins! I have cried to you,
Give me your aid,
As father and mother aid their son.
Poor, without kin or friend or ties of blood am I.
Save me before it be too late, from this my curse.

युवं रथेन विमदाय शुन्ध्युवं न्यूहथुः पुरुमित्रस्य योषणाम्।
युवं हवं वध्रिमत्या अगच्छतं युवं सुषुतिं चक्रथुः पुरन्धये॥७॥

You, mounted on your chariot brought to Vimada,
The comely maiden of Purumitra as a bride.
You came unto the calling of the weakling's dame,
And granted noble offspring to the happy wife.

युवं विप्रस्य जरणामुपेयुषः पुनः कलेरकृणुतं युवद्वयः।
युवं वन्दनमृश्यदादुदूपथुर्युवं सद्यो विश्पलामेतवे कृथः॥८॥

You gave again the vigour of his youthful life to
the sage Kali, when old age was coming nigh,
You rescued Vandana and raised him from the pit,
And in a moment gave Viśpalā power to move.

युवं ह रेभं वृषणा गुहा हितमुदैरयतं ममृवांसमश्विना।
युवमृबीसमुत तप्तमत्रय ओमन्वन्तं चक्रथुः सप्तवध्रये॥९॥

You! Aśvins Twins! Endowed with manly strength,
brought forth Rebha when hidden in
the cave and well-nigh dead,
Freed Saptavadhri, and for Atri caused the pit
heated with fire to be a pleasant resting-place.

युवं श्वेतं पेदवेऽश्विनाश्वं नवभिर्वाजैर्नवती च वाजिनम्।
चर्कृत्यं ददथुर्द्रावयत्सखं भगं न नृभ्यो हव्यं मयोभुवम्॥१०॥

On Pedu you bestowed, Aśvins!
A courser white, mighty with nine-and-ninety

varied gifts of strength, a horse to be renowned,
Who bore his friend at speed, joy-giving,
Bhaga-like to be invoked of men.

न तं राजानावदिते कुतश्चन नांहो अश्नोति दुरितं नकिर्भयम्।
यमश्विना सुहवा रुद्रवर्तनी पुरोरथं कृणुथः पत्न्या सह।।११।।

From no side, you Two Kings,
Whom none may check or stay,
Does grief, distress, or danger come upon the man.
Whom, Aśvins swift to hear,
Borne on your glowing path,
You with your Consort, make the foremost in the race.

आ तेन यातं मनसो जवीयसा रथं यं वामृभवश्चक्रुरश्विना।
यस्य योगे दुहिता जायते दिव उभे अहनी सुदिने विवस्वतः।।१२।।

Come, On that Chariot,
Which the Ṛbhus wrought for you,
The Chariot, Aśvins! that is speedier than thought,
At harnessing whereof
Heaven's Daughter springs to birth;
And from Vivasvān come auspicious Night and Day.

ता वर्तिर्यातं जयुषा वि पर्वतमपिन्वतं शयवे धेनुमश्विना।
वृकस्य चिद्वर्तिकामन्तरास्याद्युवं शचीभिर्ग्रसिताममुञ्चतम्।।१३।।

Come, Conquerors of the sundered mountain,
To our home,
Aśvins who made the cow stream milk for Śayu's sake,
You who delivered even from the wolf's deep throat,
and set again at liberty the swallowed quail.

एतं वां स्तोममश्विनावकर्मातक्षाम भृगवो न रथम्।
न्यमृक्षाम योषणां न मर्ये नित्यं न सूनुं तनयं दधानाः।।१४।।

We have prepared this laud for you, O Aśvins!
And, like the Bhṛgus, as a car have framed it,
Have decked it as a bride to meet the bridegroom,
And brought it as a son, our stay forever.

ṚV X.40
(14 mantras)

ऋषि – घोषा काक्षीवती। देवता – अश्विनौ। छन्द – जगती।

Ṛṣikā — Ghoṣā Kākṣīvatī; Devatā — Aśvins
Metre — Jagatī

रथं यान्तं कुह को ह वां नरा प्रति द्युमन्तं सुविताय भूषति।
प्रातर्यावाणं विभ्वं विशेविशे वस्तोर्वस्तोर्वहमानं धिया शमि।।१।।

Your Radiant Chariot, where goes it on its way?
Who decks it for you?
Heroes! For its happy course,
Starting at day break,
Visiting each morning every house,
Borne hitherward through prayer unto the sacrifice?

कुह स्विद्दोषा कुह वस्तोरश्विना कुहाभिपित्वं करतः कुहोषतुः।
को वां शयुत्रा विधवेव देवरं मर्यं न योषा कृणुते सधस्थ आ।।२।।

Where are you, Aśvins! In the evening?
Where at morn? Where is your halting-place?
Where rest you for the night?
Who brings you homeward,
As the widow bedward draws her husband's brother,[3]
As the bride attracts the groom?

3. This was perhaps an acceptable custom in the Vedic age in the unfortunate circumstances of the husband's death. The law of the Jews was the same. The custom is validated in *Manusmṛti* IX.68-69. It continues in some agriculture-based families. In modern times, this custom →

प्रातर्जरेथे जरणेव कापया वस्तोर्वस्तोर्यजता गच्छथो गृहम्।
कस्य ध्वस्रा भवथः कस्य वा नरा राजापुत्रेव सवनाव गच्छथः॥३॥

Early you sing forth praise as with a herald's voice,
And meet for worship,
Go each morning to the house.
Whom do you ever bring to ruin?
Unto whose libations come you,
Heroes! Like two Sons of Kings?

युवां मृगेव वारणा मृगण्यवो दोषा वस्तोर्हविषा नि ह्वयामहे।
युवं होत्रामृतुथा जुह्वते नरेषं जनाय वहथः शुभस्पती॥४॥

Even as hunters follow two wild elephants,
We with oblations call you down at morn and eve,
To folk who pay you offerings at appointed times,
Chiefs, Lords of splendour!
You bring food to strengthen them.

युवां ह घोषा पर्यश्विना यती राज्ञ ऊचे दुहिता पृच्छे वां नरा।
भूतं मे अह्न उत भूतमक्तवेऽश्वावते रथिने शक्तमर्वते॥५॥

To you, O Aśvins! Came the daughter of a King,
Ghoṣā, and said, O Heroes! This I beg of you,
Be near me in the day, be near me in the night,
Help me to gain a car-borne chieftain rich in steeds.

युवं कवी ष्ठः पर्यश्विना रथं विशो न कुत्सो जरितुर्नशायथः।
युवोर्ह मक्षा पर्यश्विना मध्वासा भरत निष्कृतं न योषणा॥६॥

O Aśvins! You are wise, as Kutsa comes to men,
Bring your car near the folk of him,

→ has been sensitively depicted by the progressive Urdu writer Rajinder Singh Bedi in his classic Urdu novel *Ek Chadar Maili si* (1965).

who sing your praise.
The bee, O Aśvins! Bears your honey in her mouth,
As the maiden carries it purified in her hand.

युवं ह भुज्युं युवमश्विना वशं युवं शिञ्जारमुशनामुपारथुः।
युवो ररावा परि सख्यमासते युवोरहमवसा सुम्नमा चके॥७॥

To Bhujyu and to Vaśa you came near with help,
O Aśvins! To Śiñjāra and to Uṣanā.
Your worshipper secures your friendship for himself.
Through your protection, I desire felicity.

युवं ह कृशं युवमश्विना शयुं युवं विधन्तं विधवामुरुष्यथः।
युवं सनिभ्यः स्तनयन्तमश्विनाप व्रजमूर्णुथः सप्तास्यम्॥८॥

Kr̥śa and Śayu you protect, you Aśvins Twins!
You Two assist the widow and the worshipper;
And you throw open, Aśvins!
Unto those who win the cattle-stall,
That thunders with its sevenfold mouth.

जनिष्ट योषा पतयत्कनीनको वि चारुहन्वीरुधो दंसना अनु।
आस्मै रीयन्ते निवनेव सिन्धवोऽस्मा अह्ने भवति तत्पतित्वनम्॥९॥

The woman has brought forth,
The Infant has appeared,
The plants of wondrous beauty
straightaway have sprung up.
To him the rivers run as down a deep descent,
And he this day becomes their master and their lord.

जीवं रुदन्ति वि मयन्ते अध्वरे दीर्घामनु प्रसितिं दीधियुर्नरः।
वामं पितृभ्यो य इदं समेरिरे मयः पतिभ्यो जनयः परिष्वजे॥१०॥

They mourn the living, cry aloud, at sacrifice,
The men have set their thoughts upon a distant cast.

A lovely thing for fathers who have gathered here,
A joy to husbands, are the wives their arms
shall clasp.

न तस्य विद्म तदु षु प्र वोचत युवा ह यद्युवत्याः क्षेति योनिषु।
प्रियोस्त्रियस्य वृषभस्य रेतिनो गृहं गमेमाश्विना तदुश्मसि।।११।।

Of this we have no knowledge.
Tell it forth to us,
how the youth rests within the chambers of the bride.
Fain would we reach the dwelling of the vigorous
Steer who loves the kine.
O Aśvins! This is our[4] desire.

आ वामगन्त्सुमतिर्वाजिनीवसू न्यश्विना हृत्सु कामा अयंसत।
अभूतं गोपा मिथुना शुभस्पती प्रिया अर्यम्णो दुर्यां अशीमहि।।१२।।

Your favouring grace has come.
You Lords of ample wealth. Aśvins!
Our longings are stored up within your hearts.
You, Lords of splendour!
Have become our twofold guard,
May we as welcome friends reach Aryaman's abode.

ता मन्दसाना मनुषो दुरोण आ धत्तं रयिं सहवीरं वचस्यवे।
कृतं तीर्थं सुप्रपाणं शुभस्पती स्थाणुं पथेष्ठामप दुर्मतिं हतम्।।१३।।

Even so, rejoicing in the dwelling-place of man,
Give hero sons and riches to the eloquent.
Make a ford, Lords of splendour,
Where men well may drink,
Remove the spiteful tree-stump standing in the path.

---

4. Ghoṣā appears to speak of herself in the plural number. She plainly expresses her wishes for marriage. Cf. R.T.H. Griffith, *The Hymns of the Ṛgveda*, vol. II p. 440.

क्व स्विदद्य कतमास्वश्विना विक्षु दस्रा मादयेते शुभस्पती।
क ईं नि येमे कतमस्य जग्मतुर्विप्रस्य वा यजमानस्य वा गृहम्।।१४।।

O Aśvins! Wonder-Workers! Lords of lustre!
Where and with what fold do you delight
yourselves today?
Who has detained them with him?
Where are they gone?
Unto what sage's, or what worshipper's abode?

2

Godhā

Godhā is the seer of *R̥V* X.134.6 (second half) and 7, a total one and half *mantras* addressed to Indra. In *Br̥haddevatā*,[1] in the list of all *r̥ṣikās*, Godhā's name is there. Ācārya Sāyaṇa has described her as a *brahmavādinī* in his *Bhāṣyam* — *pūrveṇetyardharca-sahitāyāḥ saptamyāstu godhā nāma brahmavādinyar̥ṣiḥ.*[2]

Of the one and half *mantra* attributed to Godhā in the *R̥gveda* (X.134.7) is repeated with some minor changes as *Sāmaveda* – 176 also addressed to Indra and is credited to her.

R̥V X.134

(7 mantras)

ऋषि – १-५, ६ (पूर्वार्ध) मान्धाता यौवनाश्वः, ६ (उत्तरार्ध) – ७ गोधा (ऋषिका)। देवता – इन्द्रः। छन्द – महापङ्क्तिः, ७-पङ्क्तिः।

R̥ṣi — 1-5, 1st half of 6 Māndhātā Yauvanāśva;
2nd half of 6, 7 Godhā (R̥ṣikā);
Devatā — Indra; Metre — Mahāpaṅkti, 7-Paṅkti

उभे यदिन्द्र रोदसी आपप्राथोषा इव।
महान्तं त्वा महीनां सम्राजं चर्षणीनां
देवी जनित्र्यजीजनद्भद्रा जनित्र्यजीजनत्।।१।।

As like the Morning, you have filled,
O Indra, both the earth and heaven,

1. *Br̥had.*, II.82.
2. *R̥V.Sā.Bh.*, X.134.

So as the mighty One,
Great King of all the mighty world of men,
The Goddess Mother[3] brought you forth,
The Blessed Mother gave you life.

अव स्म दुर्हणायतो मर्तस्य तनुहि स्थिरम्।
अधस्पदं तमीं कृधि यो अस्माँ आदिदेशति
देवी जनित्र्यजीजनद्भद्रा जनित्र्यजीजनत्॥२॥

Relax that mortal's stubborn strength
whose heart is bent on wickedness.
Trample him down beneath thy feet
who watches for, and aims at us.
The Goddess Mother brought you forth,
The Blessed Mother gave you life.

अव त्या बृहतीरिषो विश्वश्चन्द्रा अमित्रहन्।
शचीभिः शक्र धूनुहीन्द्र विश्वाभिरूतिभिर्देवी
जनित्र्यजीजनद्भद्रा जनित्र्यजीजनत्॥३॥

Shake down, O Slayer of the foe!
those great all-splendid energies.
With all your powers, O Śakra! all your helps,
O Indra! Shake them down;
The Goddess Mother brought you forth,
The Blessed Mother gave you life.

अव यत्त्वं शतक्रतविन्द्र विश्वानि धूनुषे।
रयिं न सुन्वते सचा सहस्रिणीभिरूतिभिर्देवी
जनित्र्यजीजनद्भद्रा जनित्र्यजीजनत्॥४॥

As You, O Śatakratu!
You, O Indra! Shakes all things down.
As wealth for him who sheds the juice,

3. Aditi.

With your assistance thousandfold.
The Goddess Mother brought you forth,
The Blessed Mother gave you life.

अव स्वेदा इवाभितो विष्वक्पतन्तु दिद्यवः।
दूर्वाया इव तन्तवो व्य१स्मदेतु दुर्मतिर्देवी
जनित्र्यजीजनद्भद्रा जनित्र्यजीजनत्।।५।।

Around, on every side like drops of sweat
let lightning-flashes fall.
Let all malevolence pass away from us,
like threads of Dūrvā[4] grass.
The Goddess Mother brought you forth,
The Blessed Mother gave you life.

दीर्घं ह्यङ्कुशं यथा शक्तिं बिभर्षि मन्तुमः।
पूर्वेण मघवन्पदाजो वयां यथा यमो
देवी जनित्र्यजीजनद्भद्रा जनित्र्यजीजनत्।।6।।

You bear in your hand a lance like a long hook,
Great Counsellor!
As with his foremost foot a goat,
draw down the branch, O Maghavan.
The Goddess Mother brought you forth,
The Blessed Mother gave you life.

नकिर्देवा मिनीमसि नकिरा योपयामसि मन्त्रश्रुत्यं चरामसि।
पक्षेभिरपिकक्षेभिरत्राभि सं रभामहे।।७।।

Never, O Gods, do we offend,
Nor are we ever obstinate:
We walk as holy texts command.
Closely we clasp and cling to you,
Cling to your sides, beneath your arms.

---

4. *panicium dactylon*, a species of bent grass whose filaments stretch horizontally away from the stem.

3

Viśvavārā Ātreyī

VIŚVAVĀRĀ Ātreyī is the seer of *ṚV* V.28 addressed to Agni containing six *mantras*. She is the daughter of Ṛṣi Atri, hence the title Ātreyī. Bṛhaddevatākāra has included her in the list of *ṛṣikās*.[1] Ācārya Sāyaṇa has also confirmed her seerhood thus — *ātreyam-anukramaṇikā 'samiddho viśvavārātreyī — iti', atri-gotrotpannā viśvavārā-nāmikā asya sūktasya ṛṣi.'*[2] Of the six *mantras* in *ṚV* V.28, the third *mantra ṚV* V.28.3 is exactly repeated *in toto* as *Yajurveda* XXXIII.12 addressed to Agni. Maharṣi Kātyāyana, in his *Sarvānukramaṇī*, describes her as — *agne śardha 'atri-duhitā viśvavārā.*[3] She is named Atri-duhitā Viśvavārā in *Yajurveda*. Ācārya Mahīdhara has presented her thus in his *Yajurveda-Bhāṣyam* — *triṣṭup viśvavārā dṛṣṭā dvitīyamarutvatīyapuroruk.*[4]

ṚV V.28

(6 mantras)

ऋषि – विश्ववारात्रेयी। देवता – अग्निः।

छन्द – १, ३ त्रिष्टुप्, २ जगती, ४ अनुष्टुप्, ५-६ गायत्री।

Ṛṣikā — Viśvavārā Ātreyī Devatā — Agni

Metre — 1, 3 Triṣṭup, 2 Jagatī, 4 Anuṣṭup, 5-6 Gāyatrī

समिद्धो अग्निर्दिवि शोचिरश्रेत् प्रत्यङ्ङुषसमुर्विया वि भाति।
एति प्राची विश्ववारा नमोभिर्देवाँ ईळाना हविषा घृताची।।१।।

1. *Bṛhad.*, II.82.
2. *ṚV.Sā.Bh.*, V.8.
3. *Sar.*, III.17.
4. *Ma.Bhā.*, XXXIII.12.

Agni inflamed has sent to heaven his lustre,
He shines forth widely turning unto Morning.
Eastward the ladle goes that brings all blessing,
Praising the Gods with homage and oblation.

समिध्यमानो अमृतस्य राजसि हविष्कृण्वन्तं सचसे स्वस्तये।
विश्वं स धत्ते द्रविणं यमिन्वस्यातिथ्यमग्ने नि च धत्त इत्पुरः।।२।।

Enkindled, You are King of the immortal world:
Him who brings offerings you attend for his weal.
He whom you urge on makes all possessions his,
He sets before you, Agni! Gifts that guests may claim.

अग्ने शर्ध महते सौभगाय तव द्युम्नान्युत्तमानि सन्तु।
सं जास्पत्यं सुयममा कृणुष्व शत्रूयतामभि तिष्ठा महांसि।।३।।

Show yourself strong for mighty bliss, O Agni!
Most excellent be your effulgent splendours.
Make easy to maintain our household lordship,
And overcome the might of those who hate us.

समिद्धस्य प्रमहसोऽग्ने वन्दे तव श्रियम्।
वृषभो द्युम्नवाँ असि समध्वरेष्विध्यसे।।४।।

Your glory Agni! I adore,
Kindled, exalted in your strength.
A Steer of brilliant splendour,
You are lighted well at sacred rites.

समिद्धो अग्न आहुत देवान्यक्षि स्वध्वर।
त्वं हि हव्यवाळसि।।५।।

Agni! Invoked and kindled, serve the Gods,
You skilled in sacrifice,
For you are the bearer of our gifts.

आ जुहोता दुवस्यताग्निं प्रयत्यध्वरे।
वृणीध्वं हव्यवाहनम्।।६।।

Invoke and worship Agni
While the sacrificial rite proceeds,
For offering-bearer choose you him.

4

Apālā Ātreyī

Apālā Ātreyī is the seer of the whole *sūkta* *Ṛ̥V* VIII.91 containing seven *mantra*s addressed to Lord Indra. She is the daughter of Ṛ̥ṣi Atri, one of the *sapta-ṛ̥ṣayaḥ*,[1] hence the adjective Ātreyī. In *Bṛ̥haddevatā* her seerhood is confirmed along with some other Ṛ̥ṣikās — *ghoṣā godhā viśvavārā apālopaniṣanniṣat*.[2] Ācārya Sāyaṇa has described her seerhood as — *atreḥ putryapālākhyā-tvagdoṣa parihārāyanena svaktenendraṁ stutavatī, ataḥ saivarṣiḥ*.[3] As per a Purāṇic story, she was forsaken by her husband after she contacted a cutaneous disease. She came back to her father's house and was very sad. She was cured of the disease after she worshipped Lord Indra. The last *mantra* of *Ṛ̥V* VIII.91 has this reference — *apālām-indra triṣpūtvyakṛ̥ṇoḥ sūrya-tvacam*. Indra cured Apālā of the three wounds and blessed her with brilliance.

'The Apālā-sūkta is generally considered as one of the hymns which do not belong to the solemn ritual with which the vast majority of Ṛ̥gvedic hymns are concerned. It is also counted among the so-called *ākhyāna* or *itihāsa*-hymns, which are based on legends'.[4]

---

1. *Sapta ṛ̥ṣayaḥ*, (i) Bharadvāja Bārhaspatya, (ii) Kaśyapa Mārica, (iii) Gotama Rāhugaṇa, (iv) Atri Bhauma, (v) Viśvāmitra Gāthina, (vi) Jamadagni Bhārgava, and (vii) Vasiṣṭha Maitrāvaruṇi.
2. *Bṛ̥had.*, II.82.
3. *Ṛ̥V.Sā.Bh.*, VIII.91.
4. Cf., 'The Affliction of Apālā' in *Some Women's Rites and Rights* by Hanns-Peter Schmidt, BORI.

Ṛ̥V VIII.91 (7 mantras)

ऋषि – अपाला आत्रेयी। देवता – इन्द्रः।
छन्द – अनुष्टुप्, १-२ पङ्क्तिः।

Ṛṣikā — Apālā Ātreyī Devatā — Indra
Metre — Anuṣṭup, 1-2 Paṅkti

कन्या३ वारवायती सोममपि स्रुताविदत्।
अस्तं भरन्त्यब्रवीदिन्द्राय सुनवै त्वा शक्राय सुनवै त्वा।।१।।

A girl, going down to the water,
has found the Soma at the stream.
Carrying (it) home, she said,
'For Indra I will, I press you,
For Śakra I will, I press you.'

असौ य एषि वीरको गृहं गृहं विचाकशत्।
इमं जम्भसुतं पिब धानावन्तं करम्भिणमपूपवन्तमुक्थिनम्।।२।।

You dear man there! Who goes,
Looking around from house to house,
Drink this (Soma) pressed with teeth,
Which is accompanied with grain, gruel,
cake and song of praise.

आ चन त्वा चिकित्सामोऽधि चन त्वा नेमसि।
शनैरिव शनकैरिवेन्द्रायेन्दो परि स्रव।।३।।

We want to comprehend you,
(but) we do not understand you,
Slowly and in gradual drops,
O Drop, flow around for Indra.

कुविच्छकत्कुवित्करत्कुविन्नो वस्यसस्करत्।
कुवित्पतिद्विषो यतीरिन्द्रेण सङ्गमामहै।।४।।

Will he not help and work for us?
Will he not make us wealthier?
Shall we, who live hating husbands,
Unite ourselves with Indra now?

इमानि त्रीणि विष्टपा तानीन्द्र वि रोहय।
शिरस्ततस्योर्वरामादिदं म उपोदरे।।५।।

O Indra! These three places, make them sprout
These which I declare,
My father's head, the corn-field,
And this part below my belly.

असौ च या न उर्वरादिमां तन्वं१ मम।
अथो ततस्य यच्छिरः सर्वा ता रोमशा कृधि।।६।।

Make all of these grow crops of hair,
The corn-field of ours,
My body and my father's head.

खे रथस्य खेऽनसः खे युगस्य शतक्रतो।
अपालामिन्द्र त्रिष्पूत्व्यकृणोः सूर्यत्वचम्।।७।।

Cleansing Apālā thrice, O Indra!!
You gave sun-like skin to her,
O Śatakratu! Drawn through the hole of chariot,
of cart, and of yoke.

5

Juhū-Brahmajāyā

JUHŪ-BRAHMAJĀYĀ (wife of Bṛhaspati) — is the seer of the whole *sūktam* *ṚV* X.109 containing seven *mantras* addressed to Viśvedevā. Bṛhaddevatākāra Ṛṣi Śaunaka has titled her as "Brahmajāyā" — *te 'vadan-vaiśvadevaṁ tu brahmajāyā juhūr-jagau.*[1] Ācārya Sāyaṇa has recognised Juhū as *brahmavādinī* in his *bhāṣyam* — *te 'vadan iti saptarcaṁ daśamaṁ sūktam, juhūrnāma brahmavādinyaṛṣiḥ brahmaputra ūrdhvanābhā nāma vā.*[2]

ṚV X.109
(7 mantras)

ऋषि – जुहू ब्रह्मजाया, ऊर्ध्वनाभा ब्राह्मः वा, देवता – विश्वेदेवाः।
छन्द – त्रिष्टुप्, ६-७ अनुष्टुप्।

Ṛṣi — Juhū-Brahmajāyā or Ūrdhvanābhā Brāhma,
Devatā — Viśvedevā; Metre — Triṣṭup, 6-7 Anuṣṭup

तेऽवदन्प्रथमा ब्रह्मकिल्बिषेऽकूपारः सलिलो मातरिश्वा।
वीळुहरास्तप उग्रो मयोभूरापो देवीः प्रथमजा ऋतेन॥१॥

These first, the boundless Sea, and Mātariśvan,
Fierce-glowing Fire, the Strong, The Bliss-bestower,
And heavenly Floods, first-born by holy Order,
Exclaimed against the outrage on Brahmā.

---

1. *Bṛhad.,* VIII.36.
2. *ṚV.Sā.Bh.,* X.109.

सोमो राजा प्रथमो ब्रह्मजायां पुनः प्रायच्छदहृणीयमानः।
अन्वर्तिता वरुणो मित्र आसीदग्निर्होता हस्तगृह्या निनाय।।२।।

King Soma first of all, without reluctance,
Made restitution of the Brahmā's consort.
Mitra and Varuṇa were the inviters,
Agni as Hotā took her hand and led her.

हस्तेनैव ग्राह्य आधिरस्या ब्रह्मजायेयमिति चेदवोचन्।
न दूताय प्रह्ये तस्थ एषा तथा राष्ट्रं गुपितं क्षत्रियस्य।।३।।

The man, her pledge, must by her hand be taken
When they have cried;
She is Brahmā's consort.
She stayed not for a herald to conduct her,
Thus is the kingdom of a ruler guarded.

देवा एतस्यामवदन्त पूर्वे सप्तऋषयस्तपसे ये निषेदुः।
भीमा जाया ब्राह्मणस्योपनीता दुर्धां दधाति परमे व्योमन्।।४।।

Thus spoke of her those Gods of old,
Seven Ṛṣis who sat them down to their austere devotion,
Dire is a Brahmā's wife led home by others,
In the supreme heaven, she plants confusion.

ब्रह्मचारी चरति वेविषद्विषः स देवानां भवत्येकमङ्गम्।
तेन जायामन्वविन्दद् बृहस्पतिः सोमेन नीतां जुह्वं१ न देवाः।।५।।

The Brahmacārī goes engaged in duty,
He is a member of the Gods' own body.
Through him, Bṛhaspati obtained him consort,
As the Gods gained the ladle brought by Soma.

पुनर्वै देवा अददुः पुनर्मनुष्या उत।
राजानः सत्यं कृण्वाना ब्रह्मजायां पुनर्ददुः।।६।।

So then, Gods restored her,
So men gave the woman back again.
The Kings who kept their promises,
Restored the Brahmā's wedded wife.

पुनर्दाय ब्रह्मजायां कृत्वी देवैर्निकिल्बिषम्।
ऊर्जं पृथिव्या भक्त्वायोरुगायमुपासते।।७।।

Having restored the Brahmā's wife,
And freed them, with gods' aid, from sin,
They shared the fullness of the earth,
And won themselves extended sway.

6

Agastya-svasā

AGASTYA-SVASĀ (sister of Agastya) is the seer of *R̥V* X.60.6 (one *mantra*), addressed to King Asamāti (here a *devatā* as per definition), in which she has asked for the defeat the miser businessman, who is not charitable for a good cause. Ācārya Sāyaṇa has described her as *ṣaṣṭhyāstvagastasya svasaiṣāṁ matarṣikā* I He has also quoted from *Anukramaṇikā* – *ṣaṣṭhyāgastasya svasā matariṣāṁ* I [1]

R̥V X.60

(12 mantras)

ऋषि – बन्धुः, सुबन्धुः, श्रुतबन्धुः, विप्रबन्धुः, गौपायनः, लौपायनः वा, ६ अगस्त्यस्वसा (ऋषिका)।

देवता – १-४, ६ असमातिः, ५ इन्द्रः, ७-११ जीवः १२ हस्तः।

छन्द – अनुष्टुप्, १-५ गायत्री, ८-९ पङ्क्तिः।

R̥ṣi — Bandhu, Subandhu, Śrutabandhu, Viprabandhu, Gaupāyana or Laupāyana, 6 Agastya-svasā (R̥ṣikā)

Devatā — 1-4, 6 Asamāti, 5 Indra, 7-11 Jīva, 12 Hasta

Metre – Anuṣṭup, 1-5 Gāyatrī, 8-9 Paṅkti

आ जनं त्वेषसन्दृशं माहीनानामुपस्तुतम्।
अगन्म बिभ्रतो नमः।।१।।

Bringing our homage,
We have come to one magnificent in look,
Glorified of the mighty Gods.

1. *R̥V. Sā.Bh.*, X.60.

असमातिं नितोशनं त्वेषं निययिनं रथम्।
भजेरथस्य सत्पतिम्।।२।।

To Asamāti, spring of gifts,
Lord of the brave, a radiant car,
The conqueror of Bhajeratha.

यो जनान्महिषाँ इवतितस्थौ पवीरवान्।
उतापवीरवान्युधा।।३।।

Who, when the spear has armed his hand,
Or even weaponless overthrows.
Men strong as buffalos in fight.

यस्येक्ष्वाकुरुप व्रते रेवान्मराय्येधते।
दिवीव पञ्च कृष्टयः।।४।।

Him in whose service flourishes Ikṣvāku,
Rich and dazzling-bright,
As the Five Tribes that are in heaven.

इन्द्र क्षत्रासमातिषु रथप्रोष्ठेषु धारय।
दिवीव सूर्यं दृशे ।।५।।

Indra, support the princely power of Rathaproṣṭha matched by none,
Even as the Sun for all to see.

अगस्त्यस्य नद्भ्यः सप्ती युनक्षि रोहिता।
पणीन्न्यक्रमीरभि विश्वन्राजन्नराधसः।।६।।

You for Agastya's sister's sons,
Yokes your pair of ruddy steeds.
You trod misers under foot,
all those, O King, who brought no gifts.

अयं मातायं पितायं जीवातुरागमत्।
इदं तव प्रसर्पणं सुबन्धवेहि निरिहि।।७।।

This is the mother, this the father,
This one has come to be your life.
What brings you forth is even this.
Now come, Subandhu, get you forth.[2]

यथा युगं वरत्रया नह्यन्ति धरुणाय कम्।
एवा दाधार ते मनो जीवातवे न मृत्यवेऽथो अरिष्टतातये।।८।।

As with the leather thong
They bind the chariot yoke to hold it fast,
So have I held your spirit fast,
Held it for life and not for death,
Held it for your security.

यथेयं पृथिवी मही दाधारेमान्वनस्पतीन्।
एवा दाधार ते मनो जीवातवे न मृत्यवेऽथो अरिष्टतातये।।९।।

Even as this earth, the mighty earth,
Holds fast the monarchs of the wood.
So have I held your spirit fast,
Held it for life and not for death,
Held it for your security.

---

2. *Mantras* 7-12 do not appear to have any connection with *mantras* 1-6. In the 7th *mantra* Subandhu is in a trance, and apparently dead. It is supposed that the brothers of Subandhu have addressed their supplications to Agni, to restore him back to life, and that he has come accordingly, being as it were, his parent and begetter. Another interpretation explains the terms literally as, "Subandhu, your father, mother, and son have come to mourn your decease."

— Wilson's explanation as in R.T.H. Griffith, *The Hymns of the Ṛgveda*, vol. II, p. 464 f.n.

यमादहं वैवस्वतात्सुबन्धोर्मन आभरम्।
जीवातवे न मृत्यवेऽथो अरिष्टतातये॥१०॥

Subandhu's spirit I have brought from Yama,
From Vivasvān's Son.
Brought it for life and not for death,
Yes, brought it for security.

न्य१ग्वातोऽव वाति न्यक्तपति सूर्यः।
नीचीनमघ्न्या दुहे न्यग्भवतु ते रपः॥११॥

The wind blows downward from on high,
Downward the Sun God sends his heat,
Downward the milch-cow pours her milk,
So downward go they pain and grief.

अयं मे हस्तो भगवानयं मे भगवत्तरः।
अयं मे विश्वभेषजोऽयं शिवाभिमर्शनः॥१२॥[3]

Felicitous is this mine hand,
Yet more felicitous is this,
This hand contains all healing balms,
And this makes whole with gentle touch.

3. This familiar *mantra* is part of Śrī Rudram.

7

Aditi or Aditi-Dākṣāyaṇī

Aditi or Aditi-Dākṣāyaṇī is the seer of *ṚV* IV.18 second half of 4, and 7 (1½ *mantras*) addressed to Vāmadeva, and *ṚV* X.72 (9 *mantras*) addressed to *Devagaṇa*. Aditi is considered the mother of the *Devatās* (Diti being the mother of all *Daityas* — the demons), and mother of Āditya.[1] Aditi has also been described severally, as the sovereign of the earth, space and the heaven.[2] In the stories about the description of Ṛṣis in the *Anukramaṇī*, Aditi is treated as the Ṛṣikā of the whole of *ṚV* IV.18 known as Vaiśvedevā-Sūktam.[3] The Hymn describes the birth and infancy of Indra. Bṛhaddevatākāra has also treated Aditi as the seer of Vaiśvadeva-Sūktam, and has introduced her as Dakṣaputrī[4] — daughter of Dakṣa.

ṚV IV.18

Vaiśvedevā-Sūktam (13 mantras)

ऋषि – वामदेवो गौतमः, १ इन्द्रः,
४ (उत्तरार्ध) ७ अदितिः (ऋषिका)।
देवता – १ वामदेवः, २-४ (पूर्वार्ध) ८-१३ इन्द्रः,
४ (उत्तरार्ध), ५,६,७ वामदेवः। छन्द – त्रिष्टुप्।

---

1. *aṣṭayoniṁ-aṣṭaputrām . . . aṣṭau putrāso aditeḥ.* — *Tai. Ār.* I.13.1-2.

2. *aditi-dyaur-aditir-antarikṣam-aditirmāta sa pitā sa putraḥ.* — *ṚVS* I.89.10.

3. *indro 'ditir-ṛṣiścāsminnithaḥ sūkte samūcire.* — *Anu.Bhā.* IV.18.

4. *partho dakṣasutāditiḥ.* — *Bṛhad.*, III.57.

Ṛṣi – Vāmadeva Gautama, 1 Indra,
2nd half of 4 and 7 Aditi-Dākṣāyaṇī (Ṛṣikā)
Devatā – 1 Vāmadeva, 2, 3, 2nd half of 4, 8-13 Indra,
4, 5 (2nd half of) 6, 7 Vāmadeva; Metre – Triṣṭup

अयं पन्था अनुवित्तः पुराणो यतो देवा उदजायन्त विश्वे।
अतश्चिदा जनिषीष्ट प्रवृद्धो मा मातरममुया पत्तवे कः।।१।।

This is the ancient and accepted pathway,
by which all Gods have come into existence.
Hereby could one be born though waxen mighty.
Let him not, otherwise, destroy his Mother.

नाहमतो निरया दुर्गहैतत्तिरश्चता पार्श्वान्निर्गमाणि।
बहूनि मे अकृता कर्त्वानि युध्यै त्वेन सं त्वेन पृच्छै।।२।।

Not this way go I forth, hard is the passage
Forth from the side will I issue
Much that is yet undone must I accomplish,
One must I combat and the other question.

परायतीं मातरमन्वचष्ट न नानु गान्यनु नू गमानि।
त्वष्टुर्गृहे अपिबत्सोममिन्द्रः शतधन्यं चम्वोः सुतस्य।।३।।

He bent his eye upon the dying Mother,
My word I now withdraw. That way I follow.
In Tvaṣṭṛ's dwelling Indra drank the Soma,
A hundred worth of juice pressed from the mortar.

किं स ऋधक्कृणवद्यं सहस्रं मासो जभार शरदश्च पूर्वीः।
नही न्वस्य प्रतिमानमस्त्यन्तर्जातेषूत ये जनित्वाः।।४।।

What strange act shall he do?
He whom his Mother bore for a thousand months,
And many autumns?
No peer has he among those born already,
Not among those who shall be born hereafter.

अवद्यमिव मन्यमाना गुहाकरिन्द्रं माता वीर्येणा न्यृष्टम्।
अथोदस्थात्स्वयमत्कं वसान आ रोदसी अपृणाज्जायमानः।।५।।

Deeming him a reproach, his Mother hid him,
Indra, endowed with all heroic valour.
Then up he sprang himself, assumed his vesture,
And filled, as soon as born the earth and heaven.

एता अर्षन्त्यललाभवन्तीर्ऋतावरीरिव संक्रोशमानाः।
एता वि पृच्छ किमिदं भनन्ति कमापो अद्रिं परिधिं रुजन्ति।।६।।

With lively motion onward-flow these waters
the Holy Ones shouting, as 'twere together.
Ask them to tell you what the floods are saying,
What girdling rock the waters burst apart.

किमु ष्विदस्मै निविदो भनन्तेन्द्रस्यावद्यं दिधिषन्त आपः।
ममैतान्पुत्रो महता वधेन वृत्रं जघन्वाँ असृजद्वि सिन्धून्।।७।।

Are they addressing him with words of welcome?
Will the floods take on them the shame of Indra?
With his great thunderbolt, my Son has slaughtered
Vṛtra, And set these rivers free to wander.

ममच्चन त्वा युवतिः परास ममच्चन त्वा कुषवा जगार।
ममच्चिदापः शिशवे ममृड्युर्ममच्चिदिन्द्रः सहसोदतिष्ठत्।।८।।

I cast you from me, mine, your youthful mother,
You, my own offspring, Kuṣavā has swallowed.
To him, mine infant, were the waters gracious
Indra, my Son, rose up in conquering vigour.

ममच्चन ते मघवन्व्यंसो निविविध्वाँ अप हनू जघान।
अधा निविद्ध उत्तरो बभूवाञ्छिरो दासस्य सं पिणग्वधेन।।९।।

Thou are mine own, O Maghavan,
Whom Vyansa struck to the ground,

And smote your jaws in pieces.
But, smitten through, the mastery you won,
And with your bolt the Dāsa's head you crushed.

गृष्टिः ससूव स्थविरं तवागामनाधृष्यं वृषभं तुम्रमिन्द्रम्।
अरीळ्हं वत्सं चरथाय माता स्वयं गातुं तन्व इच्छमानम्॥१०॥

The heifer hath brought forth the Strong,
The Mighty, the unconquerable Bull, The furious Indra.
The Mother left her unlicked Calf to wander,
Seeking himself, the path that he would follow.

उत माता महिषमन्ववेनदमी त्वा जहति पुत्र देवाः।
अथाब्रवीद् वृत्रमिन्द्रो हनिष्यन्त्सखे विष्णो वितरं वि क्रमस्व॥११॥

Then to her mighty Child the Mother turned her,
Saying, 'My son, these deities forsake you.'
Then Indra said, about to slaughter Vṛtra.
O my friend Viṣṇu! Stride full boldly forward.

कस्ते मातरं विधवामचक्रच्छयुं कस्त्वामजिघांसच्चरन्तम्।
कस्ते देवो अधि मार्डीक आसीद्यत्प्राक्षिणाः पितरं पादगृह्य॥१२॥

Who was he then, who made your Mother widow?
Who sought to slay you lying still or moving?
When by the foot your Father you took and slew,
What God was at hand to give thee comfort?

अवर्त्या शनु आन्त्राणि पेचे न देवेषु विविधे मर्डितारम्।
अपश्यं जायाममहीयमानामधा मे श्येनो मध्वा जभार॥१३॥

In deep distress, I cooked a dog's intestines.
Among the Gods I found not to comfort.
My consort I beheld in degradation.
The Falcon then brought me the pleasant Soma.

Ṛv X.72

(8 mantras)

ऋषि – बृहस्पतिः लौक्यः, बृहस्पतिराङ्गिरसो वा, अदिति दाक्षायणी (ऋषिका) वा। देवता – देवाः। छन्द – अनुष्टुप्।

Ṛṣi — Bṛhaspati Laukya, or Bṛhaspati Āṅgirasa, or Aditi-Dākṣāyaṇī (Ṛṣikā) Devatā — Devagaṇa Metre — Anuṣṭup

देवानां नु वयं जाना प्र वोचाम विपन्यया।
उक्थेषु शस्यमानेषु यः पश्यादुत्तरे युगे।।१।।

Let us with tuneful skill
proclaim these generations of the Gods,
That one may see them,
When these hymns are chanted in a future age.

ब्रह्मणस्पतिरेता सं कर्मार इवाधमत्।
देवानां पूर्व्ये युगेऽसतः सदजायत[5]।।२।।

These Brahmaṇaspati produced with blast and smelting, like a smith.
In an earlier age of Gods,
From Unmanifest sprang the Manifest.

देवानां युगे प्रथमेऽसतः सदजायत।
तदाशा अन्वजायन्त तदुत्तानपदस्परि।।३।।

In an earlier age of Gods,
From Unmanifest sprang the Manifest.
Thereafter were the regions born.
This sprang from the Productive Power.

---

5. Seeds of thoughts of the Upaniṣads are available in the Vedas. Here *asataḥ-sad-ajāyata* is the famous statement in *Chāndogya Upaniṣad*, meaning this manifest *jagat* is born out of the unmanifest.

भूर्जज्ञ उत्तानपदो भुव आशा अजायन्त।
अदितेर्दक्षो अजायत दक्षाद्वदितिः परि।।४।।

Earth sprang from the Productive Power,
The regions from the earth were born.
Dakṣa was born of Aditi,
And Aditi was Dakṣa's Child.

अदितिर्ह्यजनिष्ट दक्ष या दुहिता तव।
तां देवा अन्वजायन्त भद्रा अमृतबन्धवः।।५।।

For Aditi, O Dakṣa! She who is your Daughter,
Was brought forth.
After her, were the blessed Gods born
Sharers of immortal life.

यद्देवा अदः सलिले सुसंरब्धा अतिष्ठत।
अत्रा वो नृत्यतामिव तीव्रो रेणुरगायत।।६।।

When you, O Gods, in yonder
deep close-clasping one another stood.
Then, as of dancers, from your feet,
A thickening cloud of dust arose.

यद्देवा यतयो यथा भुवनान्यपिन्वत।
अत्रा रागुद्र आ गूळ्हमा सूर्यमजभर्तन।।७।।

When, O you Gods, like Yatis,
You caused all existing things to grow,
Then ye brought Sūrya forward
Who was lying hidden in the sea.

अष्टौ पुत्रासो अदितेर्ये जातास्तन्व१स्परि।
देवाँ उप प्रैत्सप्तभिः परा मार्त्ताण्डमास्यत्।।८।।

Eight are the Sons of Aditi,
Who from her body sprang to life.

With seven she went to meet the Gods,
She cast Mārtaṇḍa far away.

सप्तभिः पुत्रैरदितिरुप प्रैत्पूर्व्यं युगम्।
प्रजायै मृत्यवे त्वत्पुनर्मार्ताण्डमाभरत्॥९॥

So with her seven sons
Aditi went forth to meet the earlier age.
She brought Mārtaṇḍa thitherward,
To spring to life and die again.

Part II
Who Conversed with the Seers and Deities

8

Indrāṇī

Indrāṇī is the consort of Indra. In R̥V X.86, 12 out of the 23 *mantra*s are by Indrāṇī, addressed to Indra, and the whole *sūkta* R̥V X.145 (*sapatnī-bādhana*) containing six *mantra*s, are attributed to her. *Sūkta* R̥V X.86 is collectively attributed to Indra, Indrāṇī and Vr̥ṣākapi. In this *sūkta*, Indrāṇī is upset with Vr̥ṣākapi, and Indra along with Vr̥ṣākapi, is trying to pacify her. This is the free meaning; there could be more complex meaning at other levels. Of the 23 *mantras*, 12 *mantra*s (2, 3, 4, 5, 6, 9, 10, 15-18, 22) are seen by Indrāṇī. *Br̥haddevatā* names it as Vārṣākapaṁ-Sūktam.[1] Ācārya Sāyaṇa has admitted her as a *mantradraṣṭā — vr̥ṣākapirnāmendrasya putraḥ. sa cendrāṇīscaite trayaṁ saṁhatāḥ saṁvivādaṁ kr̥tavantaḥ . . . ityādyāścatasra ityekādaśarca indrānyā vākyāni. atastāsām-indraṇyar̥ṣiḥ.*[2]

R̥V X.86, Vārsākapaṁ Sūktam is repeated *in toto* as *AV* XX.119.

Sūkta R̥V X.145, is a spell to rid a jealous wife of a more favoured rival. Br̥haddevatākāra has substantiated her seerhood thus *imāṁ khanāmīti sūktaṁ indrāṇī yat svaṁ jagau.*[3] The term *bhāvavr̥ttam* seems to have been applied to this *sūkta* in *Br̥haddevatā*, since it is about herself. The sixth and the last *mantra* is intended to win her love of her husband, while the rest five are meant to get rid of a rival co-wife.

1. *Br̥had.*, VII.141.
2. *R̥V.Sā.Bh.*, X.86.
3. *Br̥had.*, VIII.55.

ṚV X.86

ऋषि – १, ८, ११-१४, १९-२१ इन्द्रः; ७, १३, २३ वृषाकपिः ऐन्द्रः; २-६, ९-१०, १५-१८, २२ इन्द्राणी (ऋषिका)। देवता - इन्द्रः। छन्द – पङ्क्तिः।

Vārṣākapaṁ-Sūktam (23 mantras)
(Indra, Indrāṇī-Vṛṣākapi-Trilogue)
Ṛṣi 1, 8, 11-14, 19-21 Indra; 7, 13, 23 Vṛṣakapi; 2-6, 9-10, 15-18, 22 Indrāṇī (Ṛṣikā)
Devatā - Indra Metre - Paṅkti

वि हि सोतोरसृक्षत नेन्द्रं देवममंसत।
यत्रामदद्वृषाकपिरर्यः पुष्टेषु मत्सखा विश्वस्मादिन्द्र उत्तरः॥१॥

Men have abstained from pouring juice,
They count not Indra as a God.
Where at the votary's store my friend Vṛṣākapi has drunk his fill. Supreme is Indra over all.

परा हीन्द्र धावसि वृषाकपेरति व्यथिः।
नो अह प्र विन्दस्यन्यत्र सोमपीतये विश्वस्मादिन्द्र उत्तरः॥२॥

You, Indra! Heedless pass by the ill
Vṛṣākapi has wrought,
Yet nowhere else, you find place
Wherein to drink the *soma* juice.
Supreme is Indra over all.

किमयं त्वां वृषाकपिश्चकार हरितो मृगः।
यस्मा इरस्यसीदु न्वर्यो वा पुष्टिमद्वसु विश्वस्मादिन्द्र उत्तरः॥३॥

What has he done to injure you,
This tawny beast Vṛṣākapi,
With whom you are so angry now?
What is the votary's foodful store?
Supreme is Indra over all.

यमिमं त्वं वृषाकपिं प्रियमिन्द्राभिरक्षसि।
श्वा न्वस्य जम्भिषदपि कर्णे वराहयुर्विश्वस्मादिन्द्र उत्तरः॥४॥

Soon may the hound who hunts the boar
Seize him the bite him in the ear.
O Indra! That Vṛṣākapi
Whom you protect as a friend.
Supreme is Indra over all.

प्रिया तष्टानि मे कपिर्व्यक्ता व्यदूदुषत्।
शिरो न्वस्य राविषं न सुगं दुष्कृते भुवं विश्वस्मादिन्द्र उत्तरः॥५॥

Kapi has marred the beautiful things,
All deftly wrought, that were my joy.
In pieces will I tear his head,
The sinner's portion shall be woe.
Supreme is Indra over all.

न मत्स्त्री सुभसत्तरा न सुयाशुतरा भुवत्।
न मत्प्रतिच्यवीयसी न सक्थ्युद्यमीयसी विश्वस्मादिन्द्र उत्तरः॥६॥

No Dame has ampler charms than I,
Or greater wealth of love's delights.
None with more ardour
Offers all her beauty to her Lord's embrace.
Supreme is Indra over all.

उवे अम्ब सुलाभिके यथेवाङ्ग भविष्यति।
भसन्मे अम्ब सक्थि मे शिरो मे वीव हृष्यति विश्वस्मादिन्द्र उत्तरः॥७॥

Mother whose love is quickly won,
I say what verily will be.
My breast, O Mother,
And my head and both my hips seem quivering.
Supreme is Indra over all.

किं सुबाहो स्वङ्गुरे पृथुष्टो पृथुजाघने।
किं शूरपत्नि नस्त्वमभ्यमीषि वृषाकपिं विश्वस्मादिन्द्र उत्तरः॥८॥

Dame with the lovely hands and arms,
With broad hair-plaits and ample hips.
Why, O you Hero's wife,
Are you angry with our Vṛṣākapi?
Supreme is Indra over all.

अवीरामिव मामयं शरारुरभि मन्यते।
उताहमस्मि वीरिणीन्द्रपत्नी मरुत्सखा विश्वस्मादिन्द्र उत्तरः॥९॥

This noxious creature looks on me
As one bereft of Hero's love.
Yet Heroes for my sons have I,
The Maruts' Friend and Indra's Queen.
Supreme in Indra over all.

संहोत्रं स्म पुरा नारी समनं वाव गच्छति।
वेधा ऋतस्य वीरिणीन्द्रपत्नी महीयते विश्वस्मादिन्द्र उत्तरः॥१०॥

From olden time,
The matron goes to feast and general sacrifice.
Mother of Heroes, Indra's Queen,
The rite's ordainer is extolled.
Supreme is Indra over all.

इन्द्राणीमासु नारिषु सुभगामहमश्रवम्।
नह्यस्या अपरं चन जरसा मरते पतिर्विश्वस्मादिन्द्र उत्तरः॥११॥[4]

So have I heard, Indrāṇī is called
The most fortunate among the married women,
For never shall her Consort die ever
Supreme is Indra over all.

4. This *mantra* *R̥V* X.86.11 is used in the Navagraha-Sūktam, addressed to Śukra.

नाहमिन्द्राणि रारण सख्युर्वृषाकपेर्ऋते।
यस्येदमप्यं हविः प्रियं देवेषु गच्छति विश्वस्मादिन्द्र उत्तरः॥१२॥

Never, Indrāṇī!
Have I joyed without my friend Vṛṣākapi,
Whose welcome offering here,
Made pure with water, goes to the Gods,
Supreme is Indra over all.

वृषाकपायि रेवति सुपुत्र आदु सुस्नुषे।
घसत्त इन्द्र उक्षणः प्रियं काचित्करं हविर्विश्वस्मादिन्द्र उत्तरः॥१३॥

Wealthy Vṛṣākapāyi!
Blessed with sons and consorts of your sons,
Indra will eat your bulls,
Your dear oblation that affects much,
Supreme is Indra over all.

उक्ष्णो हि मे पञ्चदश साकं पचन्ति विंशतिम्।
उताहमद्मि पीव इदुभा कुक्षी पृणन्ति मे विश्वस्मादिन्द्र उत्तरः॥१४॥

Fifteen in number, then,
Then, for me a score of bullocks they prepare,
And I devour the fat thereof,
They fill my belly full with food.
Supreme is Indra over all.

वृषभो न तिग्मशृङ्गोऽन्तर्यूथेषु रोरुवत्।
मन्थस्त इन्द्र शं हृदे यं ते सुनोति भावयुर्विश्वस्मादिन्द्र उत्तरः॥१५॥

Like as a bull with pointed horn,
Loud bellowing amid the herds.
Sweet to your heart, O, Indra!
Is the brew that she who tends you pours,
Supreme is Indra over all.

न सेशे यस्य रम्बतेऽन्तरा सक्थ्या३ कपृत्।
सेदीशे यस्य रोमशं निषेदुषो विजृम्भते विश्वस्मादिन्द्र उत्तरः॥१६॥

न सेशे यस्य रोमशं निषेदुष विजृम्भते।
सेदीशे यस्य रम्बतेऽन्तरा सक्थ्या३ कपृद्विश्वस्मादिन्द्र उत्तरः॥१७॥

अयमिन्द्र वृषाकपिः परस्वन्तं हतं विदत्।
असिं सूनां नवं चरुमादेधस्यान आचितं विश्वस्मादिन्द्र उत्तरः॥१८॥

O Indra!
This Vṛṣākapi has found a slain wild animal,
Dresser, and new-made pan and knife,
And wagon with a load of wood,
Supreme is Indra over all.

अयमेमि विचाकशद्विचिन्वन् दासमार्यम्।
पिबामि पाकसुत्वनोऽभि धीरमचाकशं विश्वस्मादिन्द्र उत्तरः॥१९॥

Distinguishing the Dāsa and the Ārya,
Viewing all, I go. I look upon the wise,
And drink the simple devotee's Soma juice.
Supreme is Indra over all.

धन्व च यत्कृन्तत्रं च कति स्वित्ता वि योजना।
नेदीयसो वृषाकपेऽस्तमेहि गृहाँ उप विश्वस्मादिन्द्र उत्तरः॥२०॥

The desert plains and steep descents,
How many leagues in length they spread!
Go to the nearest houses,
Go unto your home, Vṛṣākapi.
Supreme is Indra over all.

पुनरेहि वृषाकपे सुविता कल्पयावहै।
य एष स्वप्ननंशनोऽस्तमेषि पथा पुनर्विश्वस्मादिन्द्र उत्तरः॥२१॥

Turn back again Vṛṣākapi;
We both will bring you happiness.
You got homeward on your way,
along this path, that leads to sleep.
Supreme is Indra over all.

यदुदञ्चो वृषाकपे गृहमिन्द्राजगन्तन।
क्व१स्य पुल्वघो मृगः कमगञ्जनयोपनो विश्वस्मादिन्द्र उत्तरः॥२२॥

When, Indra and Vṛṣākapi,
You travelled upward to your home,
Where was that noisesome beast?
To whom went it, the beast that troubles man?
Supreme is Indra over all.

पर्शुर्ह नाम मानवी साकं ससूव विंशतिम्।
भद्रं भल त्यस्या अभूद्यस्या उदरमामयद्विश्वस्मादिन्द्र उत्तरः॥२३॥

Daughter of Manu,
Parśu bore a score of children at a birth.
Her portion verily was bliss
although her burden caused her grief.

ṚV X.145

(Sapatnī-bādhana-Upaniṣad) (6 mantras)

ऋषिका – इन्द्राणी। देवता – सपत्नीबाधनम् (उपनिषत्)।
छन्द – अनुष्टुप, ६ – पङ्क्तिः।

Ṛṣikā — Indrāṇī; Devatā — Sapatnī-bādhana
Metre — Anuṣṭup, 6-Paṅkti

इमां खनाम्योषधिं वीरुधं बलवत्तमाम्।
यया सपत्नीं बाधते यया संविन्दते पतिम्॥१॥

I dig this plant[5] out from the earth,
A powerful and most effective herb,
With which one quells the rival wife,
And gains the husband for oneself.

उत्तानपर्णे सुभगे देवजूते सहस्वति।
सपत्नीं मे परा धम पतिं मे केवलं कुरु।।२।।

Auspicious, with expanded leaves,
Sent by the Gods, victorious plant.
Blow thou the rival wife away,
And make my husband only mine.

उत्तराहमुत्तर उत्तरेदुत्तराभ्यः।
अथा सपत्नी या ममाधरा साधराभ्यः।।३।।

Stronger am I. O Stronger One,
Yes, mightier than the mightier;
And she, who is my rival wife,
Is lower than the lowest dames.

नह्यस्या नाम गृभ्णामि नो अस्मिन्रमते जने।
परामेव परावतं सपत्नीं गमयामसि।।४।।

Her very name I utter not:
She takes no pleasure in this man.
Far into distance most remote,
We drive the rival wife away.

अहमस्मि सहमानाथ त्वमसि सासहिः।
उभे सहस्वती भूत्वी सपत्नीं मे सहावहै।।५।।

5. Probably identical with *clypea hernandifolia*, a climbing plant possessing various medicinal properties., cf. R.T.H. Griffith, *The Hymns of the Rgveda*, vol. II, p. 589.

I am the conqueror, and You!
You too are victorious:
As victory attends us both
We will subdue my fellow wife.

उप तेऽधां सहमानामभि त्वाधां सहीयसा।
मामनु प्र ते मनो वत्सं गौरिव धावतु पथा वारिव धावतु।।६।।

I have gained you for vanquisher,
Have grasped you with a stronger spell.
As a cow hastens to her calf,
So let your spirit speed to me,
Hasten like water on its way.

9

Indramātaraḥ/Deva-bhaginī-samūha

INDRAMĀTARAḤ (mothers of Indra) or Deva-bhaginī-samūha, are the seers of *R̥V* X.153 addressed to Indra, comprising five *mantra*s.

Br̥haddevatākāra R̥ṣi Śaunaka has however treated the seer singularly — *indrāṇī cendramātā ca saramā. . .*[1] Ācārya Sāyaṇa has described them as *deva-bhaginī-samūha* — Sisters of the *devatā*s — *īṅkhayantīḥ iti pañcarcaṁ gāyatramaindraṁ dvitīyaṁ sūktaṁ devānāṁ svasr̥bhūtā indramātaro nāmar̥ṣikāḥ.*[2] The usage of plural form of the Seer as Indramātaraḥ is perhaps because of the term *'īṅkhayantīḥ'*. Also, since Indra's birth is celebrated in the hymn, perhaps the Seer is named Indramātaraḥ.

Two *mantra*s of this *sūkta* with minor modifications are available {(*R̥V* X.153.2=*SV* 120) and (*R̥V* X.153.1=*SV* 175)} in the *Sāmaveda*, also credited to Indramātaraḥ.

The five *mantra*s *'īṅkhayantīḥ iti pañcarcaṁ . . .'* are further repeated in the *Atharvaveda* XX.93.4-8 *in toto*. In the *Atharvaveda* Indramātaraḥ (mothers of Indra) or Deva-bhaginī-samūha is/are known as Devajāmi.

R̥V X.153

(5 mantras)

ऋषिका – इन्द्रमातरः। देवता – इन्द्रः। छन्द – गायत्री।

---

1. *Br̥had.*, II.83.
2. *R̥V.Sā.Bh.*, X.153.

Ṛṣikās-Indramātaraḥ (mothers of Indra)/ Deva-bhaginī-samūha; Devatā — Indra; Metre — Gāyatrī

ईङ्खयन्तीरपस्युव इन्द्रं जातमुपासते।
भेजानासः सुवीर्यम्।।१।।

Swaying about,
The Active Ones came nigh to Indra at his birth,
And shared his great heroic might.

त्वमिन्द्र बलादधि सहसो जात ओजसः।
त्वं वृषन्वृषेदसि।।२।।

Based upon strength and victory and power,
O Indra! Is your birth:
You, Mighty One! Are strong indeed.

त्वमिन्द्रासि वृत्रहा व्य१न्तरिक्षमतिरः।
उद् द्यामस्तभ्ना ओजसा।।३।।

You are the Vṛtra-slayer,
You, Indra! Have spread the firmament,
You have with might upheld the heavens.

त्वमिन्द्र सजोषसमर्कं बिभर्षि बाह्वोः।
वज्रं शिशान ओजसा।।४।।

You, Indra! Bear in your arms
The lightning that accords with you.
Sharpening your thunderbolt with might.

त्वमिन्द्राभिभूरसि विश्वा जातान्योजसा।
स विश्वा भुव आभवः।।५।।

You, Indra! Are prominent over all creatures in
your might, you have pervaded every place.

10

Saramā Devaśunī

ṚV X.108, containing eleven *mantra*s, is a dialogue between Saramā (a celestial female dog of Indra) and the group of *asura*s known as the Paṇis. This is famously known as *Saramā-Paṇi-Saṁvāda*. As per definition, *yasya vākyaṁ sa ṛṣi, yā tenocyate sā devatā*. Therefore, for the *ṛcā* uttered by Saramā, she is the Ṛṣikā, and the Paṇis are *devatā*s, for the *ṛcā* uttered by the Paṇis, they are the *ṛṣi*s and Saramā is the *devatā*. In this dialogue-hymn containing eleven *ṛcā*, six *ṛcā* (2, 4, 6, 8, 10-11) are attributed to Saramā and five (1, 3, 5, 7, 9) are attributed to the Paṇis. Ācārya Sāyaṇa has substantiated this viewpoint in his *bhāṣyam* — *tatra prathamā-tṛtīyādyā ayujo 'ntyāvarjitāḥ paṇīnāṁ vākyāni, atra ta ṛṣayaḥ saramā devatā. dvitīyā-caturthyādyā yuja ekādaśī ca ṣaṭ saramāyā vākyāni. atastāsu saṛṣiḥ, paṇayo devatā.*[1] *Bṛhaddevatā* describes the story in a very interesting manner.[2]

ṚV X.108

(Saramā-Paṇi-Dialogue) (11 mantras)

ऋषि – २, ४, ६, ८, १०-११ सरमा; १, ३, ५, ७, ९ पणयोऽसुराः;
देवता – २, ४, ६, ८, १०-११ पणयोऽसुराः; १, ३, ५, ७, ९ सरमा।
छन्द - त्रिष्टुप्।

Ṛṣikā — 2, 4, 6, 8, 10-11 Saramā; 1, 3, 5, 7, 9 The Paṇi/s
Devatā — 2, 4, 6, 8, 10-11 The Paṇis; 1, 3, 5, 7, 9 Saramā
Metre — Triṣṭup

---

1. *ṚV.Sā.Bh.*, 2X.108.
2. *Bṛhad.*, VIII.24-36.

किमिच्छन्ती सरमा प्रेदमानड् दूरे ह्यध्वा जगुरिः पराचैः।
कास्मेहितिः का परितक्म्यासीत्कथं रसाया अतरः पयांसि।।१।।

What wish of Saramā has brought her here?
The path leads far away to distant places.
What charge have you for us?
Where turns your journey?
How have you made your journey over Rasā's waters?

इन्द्रस्य दूतीरिषिता चरामि मह इच्छन्ती पणयो निधीन्वः।
अतिष्कदो भियसा तन्न आवत्तथा रसाया अतरं पयांसि।।२।।

I come as the appointed messenger of Indra,
Seeking your ample stores of wealth, O Paṇis!
This has preserved me from the fear of crossing,
Thus have I made my way over Rasā's waters.

कीदृङिङ्ङन्द्र सरमे का दृशीका यस्येदं दूतीरसरः पराकात्।
आ च गच्छान्मित्रमेना दधामाथा गवां गोपतिर्नो भवाति।।३।।

What is that Indra like?
What is his aspect whose envoy?
Saramā, from afar you have come?
Let him approach,
And we will show him friendship,
He shall be made the herdsman of our cattle.

नाहं तं वेद दभ्यं दभत्स यस्येदं दूतीरसरं पराकात्।
न तं गूहन्ति स्त्रवतो गभीरा हता इन्द्रेण पणयः शयध्वे।।४।।

I know him safe from harm, but he can punish,
Who sent me here from afar as envoy.
Rivers flowing with deep waters
Cannot hide Him.
Low will you lie. O Paṇis! Slain by Indra.

इमा गावः सरमे या ऐच्छः परि दिवो अन्तान्त्सुभगे पतन्ती।
कस्त एना अव सृजादयुध्व्युतास्माकमायुधा सन्ति तिग्मा॥५॥

These are the kine which, Saramā!
You seek, flying,
O Blessed One! To the ends of heaven.
Who will lose these for you without a battle?
Yes, and sharp-pointed are our warlike weapons.

असेन्या वः पणयो वचांस्यनिषव्यास्तन्वः सन्तु पापीः।
अधृष्टो व एतवा अस्तु पन्था बृहस्पतिर्व उभया न मृळात्॥६॥

Even if your wicked bodies,
O you Paṇis! Were arrow-proof,
Your words are weak for wounding,
And were the path to you as yet unmastered,
Bṛhaspati in neither case will spare you.

अयं निधिः सरमे अद्रिबुध्नो गोभिरश्वेभिर्वसुभिन्यृष्टः।
रक्षन्ति तं पणयो ये सुगोपा रेकु पदमलकमा जगन्थ॥७॥

Paved with the rock,
Is this our treasure-chamber,
Full of precious things, of kine, and horses,
These Paṇis who are watchful keepers guard it,
In vain have you approached this lonely station.

एह गमन्नृषयः सोमशिता अयास्यो अङ्गिरसो नवग्वाः।
त एतमूर्वं वि भजन्त गोनामथैतद्वचः पणयो वमन्नित्॥८॥

Ṛṣis will come spirited with Soma.
The Aṅgiras unwearied, and the Navagvas.
This stall of cattle will they part among them,
Then will Paṇis wish these words unspoken.

एवा च त्वं सरम आजगन्थ प्रबाधिता सहसा दैव्येन।
स्वसारं त्वा कृणवै मा पुनर्गा अप ते गवां सुभगे भजाम॥९॥

Even thus, O Saramā! Have you come here,
Forced by celestial might to make the journey.
Do not turn back, for you will be our sister,
O Blessed One! We will give you the cattle.

नाहं वेद भ्रातृत्वं नो स्वसृत्वमिन्द्रो विदुरङ्गिरसश्च घोराः।
गोकामा मे अच्छदयन्यदायमपात इत पणयो वरीयः॥१०॥

Brotherhood, sisterhood, I know not either,
The dread Aṅgirases and Indra know them.
They seemed to long for kine when I departed.
Hence, into distance, be you gone, O Paṇis!

दूरमित पणयो वरीय उद्गावो यन्तु मिनतीर्ऋतेन।
बृहस्पतिर्या अविन्दन्निगूळ्हाः सोमो ग्रावाण ऋषयश्च विप्राः॥११॥

Hence, far away you Paṇis!
Let the cattle lowing come forth,
As holy Law commands
Kine that Bṛhaspati and Soma, Ṛṣis, Sages,
And pressing-stones have found when hidden.

11

Romaśā

Romaśā is the daughter of Bṛhaspati and wife of King Svanaya Bhāvayavya. In the *Ṛgveda,* only one *ṛk* of *ṚV* I.126.7 addressed to Svanaya Bhāvayavya, is attributed to her. Bṛhaddevatākāra has introduced her as the daughter of Indrāṇī, and wife of King Svanaya Bhāvayavya — *prādātsutāṁ romaśāṁ nāma nāmnā bṛhaspatir-bhāvayavyāya rājñe.*[1] As a *mantradraṣṭī,* Bṛhaddevatākāra has included her name along with other Ṛṣikās.[2]

ṚV I.126

(7 mantras)

ऋषि – १-५ कक्षीवान् दैर्घतमस् औशिजः, ६ स्वनयो भावयव्यः ७ रोमशा (ऋषिका)। देवता – १-५, ७ स्वनयो भावयव्यः, ६ रोमशा। छन्द – त्रिष्टुप्, ६-७ अनुष्टुप्।

Ṛṣi — 1-5 Kakṣīvān Dairghatamas;
6 Svanaya Bhāvayavya, 7 Romaśā (Ṛṣikā)
Devatā — 1-5, 7 Svanaya Bhāvayavya, 6 Romaśā,
Metre — Triṣṭup, 6-7 Anuṣṭup

अमन्दान्स्तोमान्प्र भरे मनीषा सिन्धावधि क्षियतो भाव्यस्य।
यो मे सहस्रममिमीत सवानतूर्तो राजा श्रव इच्छमानः॥१॥

With wisdom I present these lively praises of Bhavya, dweller on the bank of Sindhu;

1. *Bṛhad.,* III.156.
2. *Bṛhad.,* II.82-84.

For he, unconquered king, desiring glory,
Has furnished me a thousand sacrifices.

शतं राज्ञो नाधमानस्य निष्कान्छतमश्वान् प्रयतान्त्सद्य आदम्।
शतं कक्षीवाँ असुरस्य गोनां दिवि श्रवोऽजरमा ततान॥२॥

A hundred necklets from the king, beseeching,
A hundred gift steeds I at once accepted;
Of the lord's cows a thousand, I, Kakṣivān.
His deathless glory has he spread to heaven.

उप मा श्यावाः स्वनयेन दत्ता वधूमन्तो दश रथासो अस्थुः।
षष्टिः सहस्रमनु गव्यमागात्सनत्कक्षीवाँ अभिपित्वे अह्नाम्॥३॥

Horses of dusky colour stood besides me,
Ten chariots, Svanaya's gift,
With mares to draw them.
Kine numbering sixty thousand followed after,
Kakṣivān gained them when the days were closing.

चत्वारिंशद्दशरथस्य शोणाः सहस्रस्याग्रे श्रेणिं नयन्ति।
मदच्युतः कृशनावतो अत्यान्कक्षीवन्त उदमृक्षन्त पज्राः॥४॥

Forty bay horses of the ten cars' master
before a thousand lead the long procession.
Reeling in joy Kakṣivān's sons and Pajra's
Have groomed the coursers decked with pearly trappings.

पूर्वामनु प्रयतिमाददे वस्त्रीन्युक्ताँ अष्टावरिधायसो गाः।
सुबन्धवो ये विश्या इव व्रा अनस्वन्तः श्रव ऐषन्त पज्राः॥५॥

An earlier gift for you have I accepted,
Eight cows, good milkers, And three harnessed horses.
Pajras, who with your wains
With your great kinsman, like troops of subjects,
Have been fain for glory.

आगधिता परिगधिता या कशीकेव जङ्गहे।
ददाति मह्यं यादुरी याशूनां भोज्या शता।।६।।

(Ille loquitur). Adhaerens, arcte adhaerens,
illa quae mustelae similes se abdidit,
multum humoren effundens,
dat mihi complexuum centum gaudia.

उपोप मे परा मृश मा मे दभ्राणि मन्यथाः।
सर्वाहमस्मि रोमशा गन्धारीणामिवाविका।।७।।

(Illa loquitur) Prope, prope accede;
molliter me tange.
Ne pute pilos corporis mei paucos esse,
tota sum villosa sicut Gandharidum ovis.[3]

3. The *mantras* X.126.6 and 7, attributed to Svanaya Bhāvayavya and Romaśā respectively, do not appear to have any connection with the earlier *mantras* and are in different metre — *anuṣṭup*. R.T.H. Griffith, *The Hymns of the Ṛgveda*, vol. I. p. 174. Incidentally in *Ṛgveda*, the concluding *mantra* of the hymns is/are mostly in a different metre.

12

Urvaśī

R̥V X.95 is famously known as *Purūravā-Urvaśī-Saṁvāda*. It is a dialogue between Purūravā and Urvaśī. As per definition, *yasya vākyaṁ sa r̥ṣi, yā tenocyate sā devatā*. Hence, for the nine *mantras* (2, 4, 5, 7, 11, 13, 15, 16 and 18) uttered by Urvaśī, she is the R̥ṣikā and Purūravā is the Devatā. For the nine *mantras* (1, 3, 6, 8, 9, 10, 12, 14 and 17) uttered by Purūravā, she is the Devatā and he is the R̥ṣi.

The dialogue contains the seeds of a legend, which is narrated in the *Śatapatha-Brāhmaṇa*, in the *Mahābhārata*, the Purāṇas, and forms the plot of the well-known drama *Vikramorvaśīyam* of Kālidāsa. According to this legend, Urvaśī, an *apsaras* or celestial nymph, has been banished to earth where she consents to live with King Purūravā on the condition that he takes care of her two pet rams, and that she never sees him unclothed. She lives with Purūravā for four years, when the Gandharvas resolve to bring her back. They steal one of the rams at night. Purūravā springs from his bed; the Gandharvas send on him a flash of magic lightning, and Urvaśī sees her husband naked. One of the two conditions of the continuance of their union is broken, and the nymph instantly vanishes. Purūravā meets her afterwards, and in vain implores her to return. At last, she relents and a son is born to them. These are the main outlines of a somewhat variously told story.

Br̥haddevatākāra has presented her as a R̥ṣikā,[1] as well as

1. *Br̥had.*, II.83.

a Devatā — *caransarasi so 'paśyad abhirūpāmivorvarśīm.*[2] Ācārya Sāyaṇa also has presented her as a R̥ṣikā as well as a Devatā — *navar̥ca ailāsya purūravaso vākyāni, atastāsāṁ sa r̥ṣiḥ, śiṣṭā navorvaśyā vākyāni, atastāsu sarṣikā, ubhayor-vākyeṣu yo 'rthaḥ pratipadyate sā devatā.*[3]

R̥V-X-95 (18 mantras)
(Purūravā-Urvaśī-Dialogue)
ऋषिका – २, ४-५, ७, ११, १३, १५-१६, १८ उर्वशी; देवता – पुरूरवा।
ऋषि – १, ३, ६, ८-१०, १२, १४, १७ – पुरूरवा;
देवता-उर्वशी। छन्द – त्रिष्टुप्।

R̥ṣikā — 2, 4, 5, 7, 11, 13, 15-16, 18 Urvaśī; Devatā-Purūravā
R̥ṣi — 1, 3, 6, 8-10, 12, 14, 17 Purūravā; Devatā - Urvaśī
Metre — Triṣṭup

हये! जाये मनसा तिष्ठ घोरे वचांसि मिश्रा कृणवावहै नु।
न नौ मन्त्रा अनुदितास एते मयस्करन् परतरे चनाहन्।।१।।

Ho there, my consort! Stay, thou fierce-souled lady,
and let us reason for a while together.
Such thoughts as these of ours,
While yet unspoken in days gone by,
Have never brought us comfort.

किमेता वाचा कृणवा तवाहं प्राक्रमिषमुषसामग्रियेव।
पुरूरवः पुनरस्तं परेहि दुरापना वात इवाहमस्मि।।२।।

What am I now to do with this your saying?
I have gone from you like the first of Mornings.
Purūravā! return you to your dwelling,
I like the wind, am difficult to capture.

---

2. *Br̥had.*, VII.151.
3. *R̥V.Sā.Bh.*, X.95.

इषुर्न श्रिय इषुधेरसना गोषाः शतसा न रंहिः।
अवीरे क्रतौ वि दविद्युतन्नोरा न मायुं चितयन्त धुनयः।।३।।

Like a shaft sent for glory from the quiver,
Or swift steed winning cattle,
Winning hundreds,
The lightning seemed to flash,
As cowards planned it.
The minstrels bleated like a lamb in trouble.

सा वसु दधती श्वशुराय वय उषो यदि वष्ट्यन्तिगृहात्।
अस्तं ननक्षे यस्मिञ्चाकन्दिवा नक्तं श्नथिता वैतसेन।।४।।

Giving her husband's father life and riches,
From near dwelling when her lover craved her,
She sought the home where she found her pleasure,
Accepting day and night her lord's embraces.

त्रिः स्म माह्नः श्नथयो वैतसेनोत स्म मेऽव्यत्यै पृणासि।
पुरूरवोऽनु ते केतमायं राजा मे वीर तन्व१स्तदासीः।।५।।

Thrice in the day did you embrace your consort,
Though coldly she received your fond caresses.
To your desires, Purūravā! I yielded,
So were you king, O Hero! Of my body.

या सुजूर्णिः श्रेणिः सुम्नआपिर्ह्रदेचक्षुर्न ग्रन्थिनी चरण्युः।
ता अञ्जयोऽरुणयो न सस्रुः श्रिये गावो न धेनवोऽनवन्त।।६।।

The maidens Sujūrni, Śreṇi, Sumne-āpi, Caraṇyu,
Granthinī, and Hradecakṣus,
These, like red kine have hastened forth,
The bright ones,
And like milch-cows have lowed in emulation.

समस्मिञ्जायमान आसत ग्ना उतेमवर्धन्नद्य१: स्वगूर्ताः।
महे यत्त्वा पुरूरवो रणायावर्धयन् दस्युहत्याय देवाः।।७।।

While he was born, the Dames sat down together,
The Rivers with free kindness gave him nurture;
And then, Purūravā! the Gods increased you for
mighty battle, to destroy the Dasyus.

सचा यदासु जहतीष्वत्कममानुषीषु मानुषो निषेवे।
अप स्म मत्तरसन्ती न भुज्युस्ता अत्रसन्रथस्पृशो नाश्वाः।।८।।

When I, a mortal, wooed to mine embraces,
these heavenly nymphs who laid aside their apparel,
Like a scared snake they fled from me in terror,
Like chariot horses when the car has touched them.

यदासु मर्तो अमृतासु निस्पृक्सं क्षोणीभिः क्रतुभिर्न पृङ्क्ते।
ता आतयो न तन्वः शुम्भत स्वा अश्वासो न क्रीळयो दन्दशानाः।।९।।

When, loving these Immortal Ones,
The mortal has conversed with the nymphs
as they allow him.
Like swans, they show the beauty of their bodies,
Like horses in their play they bite and nibble.

विद्युन्न या पतन्ती दविद्योद्भरन्ती मे अप्या काम्यानि।
जनिष्टो अपो नर्यः सुजातः प्रोर्वशी तिरत दीर्घमायुः।।१०।।

She who flashed brilliant as the falling lightning,
Brought me delicious presents from the waters,
Now from the flood be born a strong young hero,
May Urvaśī prolong her life forever!

जज्ञिष इत्था गोपीथ्याय हि दधाथ तत् पुरूरवो म ओजः।
अशासं त्वा विदुषी सस्मिन्नहन्न म आशृणोः किमभुग्वदासि।।११।।

Your birth has made me drink from earthly milch-kine,
This power, Purūravā! has you vouchsafed me,
I knew, and, warned you on that day.
You would not hear me.
What says you, when nothing avails you?

कदा सूनुः पितरं जात इच्छाच्चक्रन्नाश्रु वर्तयद्विजानन्।
को दम्पती समनसा वि यूयोदध यदग्निः श्वशुरेषु दीदयत्॥१२॥

Who will the son be born and seek his father?
Mourner-like, will he weep when first he knows him?
When shall divide the accordant wife and husband,
While fire is shining with your consort's parents?

प्रति ब्रवाणि वर्तयते अश्रु चक्रन्न क्रन्ददाध्ये शिवायै।
प्र तत्ते हिनवा यत्ते अस्मे परेह्यस्तं नहि मूर मापः॥१३॥

I will console him when his tears are falling,
He shall not weep and cry for care that blesses.
That which is yours, between us, will I send you,
Go home again, you fool, you have not won me.

सुदेवो अद्य प्रपतेदनावृत्परावतं परमां गन्तवा उ।
अधा शयीत निर्ऋतेरुपस्थेऽधैनं वृका रभसासो अद्युः॥१४॥

Your lover shall flee forth this day for ever,
To seek, without return, the farthest distance.
Then let his bed be in Destruction's bosom,
And there let fierce rapacious wolves devour him.

पुरुरवो! मा मृथा मा प्र पप्तो मा त्वा वृकासो अशिवास उ क्षन्।
न वै स्त्रैणानि सख्यानि सन्ति सालावृकाणां हृदयान्येता॥१५॥

No, do not die, Purūravā, nor vanish,
Let not the evil-omened wolves devour you.

With women, there can be no lasting friendship:
Hearts of hyenas are the hearts of women.

सद्विरूपाचरं मर्त्येष्ववसं रात्रीः शरदश्चतस्रः।
घृतस्य स्तोकं सकृदह्न आश्नां तादेवेदं तातृपाणा चरामि।।१६।।

When amid men in altered shape I sojourned,
And through four autumns spent the nights among them.
I tasted once a day a drop of butter,
And even now with that am I contented.

अन्तरिक्षप्रां रजसो विमानीमुप शिक्षाम्युर्वशीं वसिष्ठः।
उप त्वा रातिः सुकृतस्य तिष्ठान्नि वर्तस्व हृदयं तप्यते मे।।१७।।

I, her best love, call Urvaśī to meet me,
Her, who fills air and measures out the region.
Let the gift brought by piety approach you.
Turn you to me again, my heart is troubled.

इति त्वा देवा इम आहुरैळ यथेमेतद्भवसि मृत्युबन्धुः।
प्रजा ते देवान् हविषा यजाति स्वर्ग उ त्वमपि मादयासे।।१८।।

Thus speak these Gods to you, O son of Iḷā!
As death has verily got you for his subject,
Your sons shall serve the Gods with their oblation,
And you, moreover, shall rejoice in *svarga*.

13

Lopāmudrā

Lopāmudrā is the wife of Ṛṣi Agastya Maitrāvaruṇi, one of the *saptarṣis*. She is a Ṛgvedic as well as a Yajurvedic[1] Ṛṣikā. She is the seer of the first two *ṛcā* of *ṚV* I.179, containing six *ṛcā*. The initial four *ṛcā* of *ṚV* I.179 addressed to Rati, is an intimate conversation between her and Ṛṣi Agastya. As the legend goes, Lopāmudrā was created by Ṛṣi Agastya and was given to the king of Vidarbha as a daughter. The royal couple gave her the best possible education and brought her up amidst luxury. When she attained marriageable age, Agastya, the sage who was under vows of celibacy and poverty, wanted to marry her. Lopāmudrā agreed to marry him, and left her palace for Agastya's hermitage. After serving her husband faithfully for a long period, she grew tired of the austere practice. She expressed her feelings in two stanzas (*ṛcā*) seeking his attention and love. Soon afterwards, the sage realised his duties towards his wife and obliged her. A son was born to them. He was named Dṛdhasyu, who later became a great poet.

The concluding two *ṛcā* are by Agastya's disciple, a *brahmacārī*. Lopāmudrā's name is distinctly available in the fourth *ṛk* uttered by Ṛṣi Agastya. Bṛhaddevatākāra has explained the whole situation of this *sūkta* in *Bṛhad*. IV.57-59. Ācārya Sāyaṇa has also confirmed Lopāmudrā's seerhood in his *Bhāṣyam* — *atra trayāṇāṁ dvṛcāṇāṁ lopāmudrāgastya-tacchiṣyeir-dṛṣṭatvātta evarṣayaḥ*.[2]

1. See p. 127.
2. *ṚV.Sā.Bh.*, I.179.

Lopāmudrā is also the seer of *Yajurveda-kāṇḍikā*s XVII.11-15 (11, 12, 15 addressed to Agni and 13, 14 addressed to the Prāṇa), and XXXVI.20 addressed to Agni. *Sarvānukramaṇī* presents her as — *namaste bṛhatīm-āgneyīm-ṛṣisutā lopāmudrā.*[3] Ācārya Mahīdhara has clarified further in his *Śukla-Yajurveda-Bhāṣyam: āgneyī bṛhatī lopāmudrā dṛṣṭā.*[4]

ṚV I.179 (6 mantras)
(Agastya-Lopāmudrā Dialogue)
ऋषि – १-२ लोपामुद्रा ३-४ अगस्त्यो मैत्रावरुणिः
५-६ अगस्त्यशिष्यो ब्रह्मचारी। देवता – रतिः
छन्द – त्रिष्टुप्ः, ५ बृहती।

Ṛṣi — 1-2 Lopāmudrā (Ṛṣikā), 3-4 Agastya,
5-6 Brahmacārī Devatā — Rati
Metre — Triṣṭup, 5 Bṛhatī

पूर्वीरहं शरदः शश्रमाणा दोषा वस्तोरुषसो जरयन्तीः।
मिनाति श्रियं जरिमा तनूनामप्यू नु पत्नीर्वृषणो जगम्युः।।१।।

Through many autumns have I toiled and laboured,
at night and more,
Through age-inducing dawnings.
Old age impairs the beauty of our bodies.
Let husbands still come near unto their spouses.

ये चिद्धि पूर्व ऋतसाप आसन्त्साकं देवेभिरवदन्नृतानि।
ते चिदवासुर्नह्यन्तमापुः समू नु पत्नीर्वृषभिर्जगम्युः।।२।।

For even the men aforetime, law-fulfillers,
Who with the Gods declared eternal statutes,
They have decided, but have not accomplished:
So now let wives come near unto their husbands.

3. *Sar.*, II.24.
4. *ŚYV.Ma.Bh.*, XVII-11.

न मृषा श्रान्तं यदवन्ति देवा विश्वा इत्स्पृधो अभ्यश्नवाव।
जयावेदत्र शतनीथमाजिं यत्सम्यञ्चा मिथुनावभ्यजाव।।३।।

Non inutilic est labor cui Dii favent,
nos omnes aemulos et aemulas vincamus.
Superemus in hac centum artium pugna in qua duas partes convenientes utrinque commovemus.
(Latin version)

नदस्य मा रुधतः काम आगन्नित आजातो अमुतः कुतश्चित्।
लोपामुद्रा बृषणं नी रिणाति धीरमधीरा धयति श्वसन्तम्।।४।।

Cupido me cepit illius tauri (viri) qui me despict,
utrum hinc utrum illinc ab aliqua parte nata sit.
Lopamudra taurum (maritum suum) ad se detrahit;
insipiens, illa sapientem anhelantem absorbet.
(Latin version)

इमं नु सोममन्तितो हृत्सु पीतमुप ब्रुवे।
यत्सीमागश्चकृमा तत् सु मृळतु पुलुकामो हि मर्त्यः।।५।।

This Soma I address that is most near us,
That, which has been imbibed within the spirit.
To pardon any sins we have committed,
Verily mortal man is full of longings.

अगस्त्यः खनमानः खनित्रैः प्रजामपत्यं बलमिच्छमानः।
उभौ वर्णावृषिरुग्रः पुपोष सत्या देवेष्वाशिषो जगाम।।६।।

Agastya thus, toiling with strong endeavour,
wishing for progeny and power,
Cherished, a sage of mighty strength, both classes,
And with the gods obtaind his prayer's fulfilment.

14

Nadyaḥ — The Rivers

R̥V III.33 popularly known as *Viśvāmitra-Nadī-Saṁvāda* is a dialogue between R̥ṣi Viśvāmitra and R̥ṣikā Nadyaḥ (two rivers — the Vipāṭ[1] and the Śutudrī[2]) who are regarded severally as the R̥ṣis or seers of the *mantras* ascribed to them. The legend cited by Sāyaṇa says that, Viśvāmitra, the *purohita* or the family priest of King Sudās, having obtained wealth after officiating at the king's sacrifice, came to the confluence of rivers, the Vipāṭ and the Śutudrī. Others followed. In order to make the rivers fordable, he lauded them with the first three *mantras*. The hymn has some poetical beauty, and is interesting as a relic of the traditions of the Āryans regarding their progress eastward in the Land of Five Rivers.

As per the definition, *yasya vākyaṁ sa r̥ṣi*, the rivers become the R̥ṣikās.

R̥V III.33 (13 mantras)

ऋषि – १-३, ५, ७, ९, ११-१३ विश्वामित्रः गाथिनः, ४, ६, ८, १० – नद्यः (ऋषिकाः)। देवता – १-३, ५, ९, ११-१३ नद्यः, ४, ८, १० विश्वामित्रः, ६, ७ इन्द्रः। छन्द – त्रिष्टुप्, १३ अनुष्टुप्।

---

1. The modern Beas that rises in the Himalayas and falls into the Sutlej.
2. A little to the south-east of Amritsar in Punjab.

(Viśvāmitra-Nadī-Dialogue)

Ṛṣi — 1-3, 5, 7, 9, 11-13 Viśvāmitra

4, 6, 8, 10 The Rivers (Ṛṣikā),

Devatā — 1-3, 5, 9, 11-13 Rivers; 4, 8, 10 Viśvāmitra,

6-7 Indra; Metre – Triṣṭup, 13 Bṛhatī

प्र पर्वतानामुशती उपस्थादश्वेइव विषिते हासमाने।
गावेव शुभ्रे मातरा रिहाणे विपाट्छुतुद्री पयसा जवेते।।१।।

From the bosom of the mountains
(longing to reach the ocean),
Like two eager swift mares with loosened reins,
Like two bright mother cows, licking,
Vipāṭ and Śutudrī flow down rapidly with their waters.

इन्द्रेषिते प्रसवं भिक्षमाणे अच्छा समुद्रं रथ्येव याथः।
समाराणे ऊर्मिभिः पिन्वमाने अन्या वामन्यामप्येति शुभ्रे।।२।।

Impelled by Indra, seeking acceleration
(you two) are approaching the ocean like two charioteers.
Flowing together, swelling with torrents,
each of you flow into the other, O beautiful ones!

अच्छा सिन्धुं मातृतमामयासं विपाशमुर्वीं सुभगामगन्म।
वत्सिमिव मातरा संरिहाणे समानं योनिमनु सञ्चरन्ती।।३।।

I have approached the most maternal river (Śutudrī).
We have approached the broad and beautiful Vipāśā,
Like the two mothers licking their calf,
Flowing along a common bed.

एना वयं पयसा पिन्वमाना अनु योनिं देवकृतं चरन्तीः।
न वर्तवे प्रसवः सर्गतक्तः किंयुर्विप्रो नद्यो जोहवीति।।४।।

We (as such are), swelling with this torrent
flowing in a common bed fashioned by God (Indra).
Our torrent rushing with its natural urge,
Is not to be stopped.
With what desire the Bard invokes so frequently?

रमध्वं मे वचसे सोम्याय ऋतावरीरुप मूहूर्तमेवैः।
प्र सिन्धुमच्छा बृहती मनीषावस्युरह्वे कुशिकस्य सूनुः।।५।।

O Holy Waters! Rest a moment in your journey,
in deference to my hymn sublime with Soma.
With a sublime hymn, desirous of (our) protection,
(I) Kuśika's son, have invoked the river (Śutudrī).

इन्द्रो अस्माँ अरदद्वज्रबाहुरपाहन्वृत्रं परिधिं नदीनाम्।
देवोऽनयत्सविता सुपाणिस्तस्य वयं प्रसवे याम उर्वीः।।६।।

The thunder-armed Indra dragged us out.
He destroyed Vṛtra, who stayed our currents.
Beautiful-handed god Savitā led us.
And at his command we flow, broad as we are.

प्रवाच्यं शश्वधा वीर्य१तदिन्द्रस्य कर्म यदहिं विवृश्चत्।
वि वज्रेण परिषदो जघानायन्नापोऽयनमिच्छमानाः।।७।।

That heroic deed of Indra must be lauded forever,
That he rent the dragon Ahi into pieces.
He smote away the obstructers (of waters) with his thunderbolt.
And the Waters flowed seeking their course.

एतद्वचो जरितर्मापि मृष्ठा आ यत्ते घोषानुत्तरा युगानि।
उक्थेषु कारो प्रति नो जुषस्व मा नो नि कः पुरुषत्रा नमस्ते।।८।।

O Singer! Never forget this word of yours,
(so) that (people) future generations may hear it.

O Bard! In prayers be favourable to us.
Do not make us humble among people.
We bow down to you.

ओ षु स्वसारः कारवे शृणोत ययौ वो दूरादनसा रथेन।
नि षू नमध्वं भवता सुपारा अधो अक्षाः सिन्धवः स्रोत्याभिः।।९।।

O Fair Sisters! Listen to the bard who comes to you
from faraway with cart and chariot.
Please bend down; be easy to be traversed,
Stay, Rivers!
With your streams (reaching) our axles.

आ ते कारो शृणवामा वचांसि ययाथ दूरादनसा रथेन।
नि ते नंसै पीप्यानेव योषा मर्यायेव कन्या शश्वचै ते।।१०।।

O Poet! Yes, we listen to your words,
(since) you have come from afar with cart and chariot.
For you, I bend down, like a nursing mother
(for her child),
and as a maiden yields to her lover for embrace.

यदङ्ग त्वा भरताः सन्तरेयुर्गव्यन्ग्राम इषित इन्द्रजूतः।
अर्षादह प्रसवः सर्गतक्त आ वो वृणे सुमतिं यज्ञियानाम्।।११।।

O (Rivers)! Since you have allowed me so,
may the Bharatas cross (the rivers);
May the caravan (of the Bharatas) seeking to cross
allowed (by you), and sped by Indra.
Then may your torrents flow rushing in its rapid motion.
I seek the favour of holy ones.

अतारिषुर्भरता गव्यवः समभक्त विप्रः सुमतिं नदीनाम्।
प्र पिन्वध्वमिषयन्तीः सुराधा आ वक्षणाः पृणध्वं यात शीभम्।।१२।।

The Bharatas, seeking to cross the waters have crossed,
The poet has won the favour of the Rivers.

(You) swelling with your excellent riches,
bring food, move forth in your bed,
overflow, move swiftly.

उद्व ऊर्मिः शम्या हन्त्वापो योक्त्राणि मुञ्चत।
मादुष्कृतौ व्येनसाघ्न्यौ शूनमारताम्॥१३॥

Let your torrent strike up the yoke-pins (from below),
let the waters spare the yokes.
Let not (the rivers) harmless and sinless not waste away,
may you prosper.

15

Yamī Vaivasvatī

YAMĪ Vaivasvatī (twin sister of Yama) — Seven *mantras* (1, 3, 5, 7, 9, 11, 13) of *ṚV* X.10, known as *Yama-Yamī-Saṁvāda* addressed to Yama, and *ṚV* X.154, (known as a Funeral Hymn) with 5 *mantras* are attributed to her. Being the daughter of Vivasvān, she has the title Vaivasvatī (*apatya-vācaka*).[1]

1. Commentators have glossed over the content of the Yama-Yamī-dialogue. After searching for years, I got the explanation which goes as follows — Yamī, the twin sister of Yama is regarded as the first of women, while her brother as the first of men born to Vivasvat (the Sun) and Saraṇyu, before Saraṇyu became afraid of her glorious husband. Yamī entreated her brother Yama to become her husband, as there were no others to perpetuate the human race. But Yama refused and died. Her sorrow at his loss was so great that to assuage her, the gods created night. Cf. Devi Chand, *The Yajurveda* Glossary and Index, p. 451.

   I found the explanation in another book — The idea of primal incest is unavoidable in any creation story. Bards often cringe with embarrassment as they narrate the tale of the one who appeared first in the cycle of life and the one who came second. The second is offspring, if born of the first. The second is sibling, if born with the first. Either way, it is incest. Cf. Devdutt Pattanaik, *The Goddess in India*, Inner traditions, Rochester, Vermont, page, 12.

ṚV X.10 (14 mantras)
(Yama-Yamī-Dialogue)

ऋषिका – १, ३, ५, ७, ९, ११, १३ यमी वैवस्वती। देवता – यमः।
ऋषिः – २, ४, ६, ८, १०, १२, १४ यमः। देवता – यमी वैवस्वती।
छन्द – त्रिष्टुप्, १३ विराट्स्थाना।

Ṛṣi — 1, 3, 5, 7, 9, 11, 13 Yamī Vaivasvatī (Ṛṣikā),
2, 4, 6, 8, 10, 12, 14 Yama Vaivasvata;
Devatā — Reciprocal; Metre — Triṣṭup, 13- Virāṭsthānā

ओ चित्सखायं सख्या ववृत्यां तिरः पुरू चिदर्णवं जगन्वान्।
पितुर्नपातमा दधीत वेधा अधि क्षमि प्रतरं दीध्यानः।।१।।

Fain would I win my friend
To kindly friendship. So may the Sage,
Come through the air's wide ocean,
Remembering the earth and days to follow,
Obtain a son, the issue of his father.

न ते सखा सख्यं वष्ट्येतत्सलक्ष्मा यद्विषुरूपा भवाति।
महस्पुत्रासो असुरस्य वीरा दिवो धर्तार उर्विया परि ख्यन्।।२।।

Thy friend loves not the friendship,
Which considers her who is near in kindred,
As a stranger.
Sons of the mighty Asura, the Heroes,
Supporters of the heavens,
see far around them.

उशन्ति घा ते अमृतास एतदेकस्य चित्त्यजसं मर्त्यस्य।
नि ते मनो मनसि धाय्यस्मे जन्युः पतिस्तन्व१मा विविश्याः।।३।।

Yes, this the Immortals seek of you with longing,
progeny of the sole existing mortal.
Then let your soul and mine be knit together,
and as a loving husband take your consort.

न यत्पुरा चकृमा कद्ध नूनमृता वदन्तो अनृतं रपेम।
गन्धर्वो अप्स्वप्या च योषा सा नो नाभिः परमं जामि तन्नौ।।४।।

Shall we do now what we never did before?
We who spoke righteously now talk impurely.
Gandharva in the floods, the Dame of Waters,
Such is our bond, such our most lofty kinship.

गर्भे नु नौ जनिता दम्पती कर्देवस्त्वष्टा सविता विश्वरूपः।
नकिरस्य प्र मिनन्ति व्रतानि वेद नावस्य पृथिवी उत द्यौः।।५।।

Even in the womb God Tvaṣṭā, the Vivifier,
Shaping all forms, Creator, made us consorts.
None violates his holy ordinances,
That we are his, The heavens and earth acknowledge.

को अस्य वेद प्रथमस्याह्नः क ईं ददर्श क इह प्र वोचत्।
बृहन्मित्रस्य वरुणस्य धाम कदु ब्रव आहनो वीच्या नॄन्।।६।।

Who knows that earliest day whereof you speak?
Who has beheld it? Who can here declare it?
Great is the Law of Varuṇa and Mitra,
What, wanton! Will you say to men to tempt them?

यमस्य मा यम्यं१ काम आगन्त्समाने योनौ सहशेय्याय।
जायेव पत्ये तन्वं रिरिच्यां वि चिद्वृहेव रथ्येव चक्रा।।७।।

I, Yamī, am possessed by love of Yama,
That I may rest on the same couch beside him.
I as a wife would yield me to my husband.
Like car-wheels let us speed to meet each other.

न तिष्ठन्ति न नि मिषन्त्येते देवानां स्पश इह ये चरन्ति।
अन्येन मदाहनो याहि तूयं तेन वि वृह रथ्येव चक्रा।।८।।

They stand not still, They never close their eyelids,
Those sentinels of Gods who wander round us.

Not me, go quickly, wanton with another,
And hasten like a chariot wheel to meet him.

रात्रीभिरस्मा अहभिर्दशस्येत् सूर्यस्य चक्षुर्मुहुरुन्मिमीयात्।
दिवा पृथिव्या मिथुना सबन्धू यमीर्यमस्य बिभृयादजामि।।९।।

May Sūrya's eye with days and nights endow him,
And ever may his light spread out before him.
In heaven and earth the kindred Pair co-mingle.
On Yamī be the unbrotherly act of Yama.

आ घा ता गच्छानुत्तरा युगानि यत्र जामयः कृणवन्नजामि।
उप बर्बृहि वृषभाय बाहुमन्यमिच्छस्व सुभगे! पतिं मत्।।१०।।

Sure there will come succeeding times,
When brothers and sisters will do acts
Unsuitable for kinsfolk.
Not me, O fair one! Seek another husband,
And make your arm a pillow for your consort.

किं भ्रातासद्यदनाथं भवाति किमु स्वसा यन्निर्ऋतिर्निगच्छात्।
काममूता बह्वे३ तद्रपामि तन्वा मे तन्वं१ सं पिपृग्धि।।११।।

Is he a brother when no lord is left her?
Is she a sister when Destruction comes?
Forced by my love these many words I utter.
Come near, and hold me in your close embraces.

न वा उ ते तन्वा तन्वं१ सं पपृच्यां पापमाहुर्यः स्वसारं निगच्छात्।
अन्येन मत्प्रमुदः कल्पयस्व न ते भ्राता सुभगे वष्ट्येतत्।।१२।।

I will not fold my arms about your body,
They call it sin when one comes near his sister.
Not me, prepare thy pleasures with another:
Your brother seeks not this from thee, O fair one!

बतो बतासि यम नैव ते मनो हृदयं चाविदाम।
अन्या किल त्वां कक्ष्येव युक्तं परि ष्वजाते लिबुजेव वृक्षम्।।१३।।

Alas! You are indeed a weakling, Yama!
We find in you no trace of heart or spirit.
As round the tree the woodbine clings,
Another will cling about your girt as with a girdle.

अन्यमू षु त्वं यम्यन्य उ त्वां परि ष्वजाते लिबुजेव वृक्षम्।
तस्य वा त्वं मन इच्छा स वा तवाधा कृणुष्व संविदं सुभद्राम्।।१४।।

Embrace another, Yami! Let another,
Even as the woodbine rings the tree, enfold you.
Win you his heart and let him win your fancy,
And he shall form with you a blessed alliance.

ṚV X.154

(5 mantras) (Funeral Hymn)

ऋषि – यमी वैवस्वती।

देवता – भाववृत्तम्। छन्द – अनुष्टुप्।

Ṛṣikā — Yamī Vaivasvatī

Devatā — Bhāvavṛtta; Metre — Anuṣṭup

सोम एकेभ्यः पवते घृतमेक उपासते।
येभ्यो मधु प्रधावति ताँश्चिदेवापि गच्छतात्।।१।।

For some is Soma purified,
Some sit by sacrificial oil:
To those for whom the honey flows forth,
Even to those let him depart.

तपसा ये अनाधृष्यास्तपसा ये स्वर्ययुः।
तपो ये चक्रिरे महस्ताँश्चिदेवापि गच्छतात्।।२।।

Invincible through Fervour,
Those whom Fervour has advanced to heaven.

Who showed great Fervour in their lives,
Even to those let him depart.

ये युध्यन्ते प्रधनेषु शूरासो ये तनूत्यजः।
ये वा सहस्रदक्षिणास्ताँश्चिदेवापि गच्छतात्।।३।।

The heroes who contend in war,
And boldly cast their lives away.
Or who give gift thousand flood,
Even to those let him depart.

ये चित्पूर्व ऋतसाप ऋतावान ऋतावृधः।
पितृन्तपस्वतो यम ताँश्चिदेवापि गच्छतात्।।४।।

Yes, the first followers of Law,
Law's pure and holy strengtheners.
The Fathers, Yama! Fervour-moved,
Even to those let him depart.

सहस्रणीथाः कवयो ये गोपायन्ति सूर्यम्।
ऋषीन् तपस्वतो यम तपोजाँ अपि गच्छतात्।।५।।

Skilled in a thousand ways and means,
The sages who protect the Sun.
The Ṛṣis, Yama! Fevour-moved,
Even to those let him depart.

16

Śaśvatī Āṅgirasī

Śaśvatī Āṅgirasī is the seer of *R̥V* VIII.1.34, the one *mantra* addressed to her husband Āsaṅga Plāyogi. She is the daughter of R̥ṣi Aṅgiras, hence the title Āṅgirasī (*apatya-vācaka*). Once her husband lost his virility and got it back only after R̥ṣi Medhātithis' prayers, and pleased her. After this, Śāśvatī has praised him through *r̥k* *R̥V* VIII.1.34. Ācārya Sāyaṇa has confirmed her seerhood thus — *asyāsaṅgasya bhāryāṅgirasaḥ sutā śaśvatākhyā bhartuḥ puṁstvaṁ-upalabhya prītā satī svabhartāram-anvasya sthūram-ityanayā stutavatī, atastasyā r̥cāḥ śaśvatyr̥ṣikā.*[1] Br̥haddevatākāra has also confirmed her seerhood thus — *yamī nārī ca śaśvatī*[2] *. . . tuṣṭāvāṅgirasi nārī vasantī śaśvatī patim.*[3]

R̥V VIII.1

ऋषि – १-२ प्रगाथ(घौरः)काण्वः,
३-२९ मेधातिथि-मेध्यातिथी काण्वौ, ३०-३३ आसङ्गःप्लायोगि,
३४ शश्वती आङ्गिरसी (ऋषिका)।
देवता – इन्द्रः, ३०-३४ आसङ्गःप्लायोगि
छन्द – १-४ (विषमा बृहती, समासतो बृहती),
५-३२ बृहती, ३३-३४ त्रिष्टुप्।

R̥V VIII.1
(34 mantras)
R̥ṣi — 1-2 Pragātha Ghaura Kāṇva,

1. *R̥V.Sā.Bh.*, VIII.1.
2. *Br̥had.*, II.83.
3. *Br̥had.*, VI.40.

3-29 Medhyātithi Kāṇva, 30-33 Āsaṅga Plāyogi, 34 - Śaśvatī Āṅgirasī (Ṛṣikā)
Devatā — Indra 30-34 Āsaṅga Plāyogi
Metre — 1-4 (Odd - Bṛhatī, Even - Sato Bṛhatī), 5-32 Bṛhatī, 33-34 Triṣṭup

मा चिदन्यद् वि शंसत सखायो मा रिषण्यत।
इन्द्रमित्स्तोता वृषणं सचा सुते मुहुरुक्था च शंसत॥१॥

Glorify naught besides, O friends,
So shall no sorrow trouble you.
Praise only mighty Indra when the juice is shed,
And say your lauds repeatedly.

अवक्रक्षिणं वृषभं यथाजुरं गां न चर्षणीसहम्।
विद्वेषणं संवननोभयङ्करं मंहिष्ठमुभयाविनम्॥२॥

Even him, eternal,
Like a bull who rushes down men's Conqueror, bounteous like a cow;
Him who is cause of both, of enmity and peace,
To both sides most generous.

यच्चिद्धि त्वा जना इमे नाना हवन्त ऊतये।
अस्माकं ब्रह्मेदमिन्द्र भूतु तेऽहा विश्वा च वर्धनम्॥३॥

Although these men in sundry ways invoke you to obtain your aid,
Be this our prayer, addressed, O Indra!
Unto you, your exaltation everyday.

वि तर्तूर्यन्ते मघवन् विपश्चितोऽर्यो विपो जनानाम्।
उप क्रमस्व पुरुरूपमा भर वाजं नेदिष्ठमूतये॥४॥

Those skilled in song. O Maghavan!
Among these men overcome with might,

The foeman's songs.
Come here, bring us strength in many a varied form,
most near that it may succour us.

महे चन त्वामद्रिवः परा शुल्काय देयाम्।
न सहस्राय नायुताय वज्रिवो न शताय शतामघ।।५।।

O Caster of the Stone!
I would not sell thee for a mighty price,
Not for a thousand, Thunderer!
nor ten thousand, nor a hundred,
Lord of countless wealth!

वस्याँ इन्द्रासि मे पितुरुत भ्रातुरभुञ्जतः।
माता च मे छदयथः समा वसो वसुत्वनाय राधसे।।६।।

O Indra! You are more to me
than father or miser brother is.
You and my mother, O Good Lord!
Appear alike, to give me wealth abundantly.

क्वेयथ क्वेदसि पुरुत्रा चिद्धि ते मनः।
अलर्षि युध्म खजकृत् पुरन्दर प्र गायत्रा अगासिषुः।।७।।

Where are you? Where are you gone?
For many a place attract your mind.
Haste, Warrior! Fort-destroyer!
Lord of battle's noise, haste,
Holy songs have sounded forth.

प्रास्मै गायत्रमर्चत वावातुर्यः पुरन्दरः।
याभिः काण्वस्योप बर्हिरासदं यासद्वज्री भिनत्पुरः।।८।।

Sing out the hymn to him
who breaks down castles for his faithful friend.

Verses to bring the Thunderer,
To destroy the forts,
And sit on Kāṇva's secred grass.

ये ते सन्ति दशग्विनः शतिनो ये सहास्रिणः।
अश्वासो ये ते वृषणो रघुद्रुवस्तेभिर्नस्तूयमा गहि।।९।।

The Horses that are yours in tens,
in hundreds, yes, in thousands yours,
Even those vigorous steeds,
Galloping in the course,
With those come quickly near to us.

आ त्व१द्य सबर्दुघां हुवे गायत्रवेपसम्।
इन्द्रं धेनुं सुदुघामन्यामिषमुरुधारामरङ्कृतम्।।१०।।

This day I call Śabardughā,
Who animates the holy song,
Indra the richly-yielding Milch-cow,
Who provides unfailing food in ample stream.

यत्तुदत् सूर एतशं वङ्कू वातस्य पर्णिना।
वहत् कुत्समार्जुनेयं शतक्रतुस्त्सरद् गन्धर्वमस्तृतम्।।११।।

When Sūra wounded Etaśa,
With Vāta's rolling winged car,
Indra bore Kutsa Ārjuneya off,
And mocked Gandharva, the unconquered One.

य ऋते चिदभिश्रिषः पुरा जत्रुभ्य आतृदः।
सन्धाता संधिं मघवा पुरूवसुरिष्कर्ता विह्रुतं पुनः।।१२।।

He without ligature,
Before making incision in the neck,
Closed up the wound again,
Most wealthy Maghavan,
Who makes whole the injured part.

मा भूम निष्ट्या इवेन्द्र त्वदरणा इव।
वनानि न प्रजहितान्यद्रिवो दुरोषासो अमन्महि॥१३॥

May we be never cast aside,
And strangers, as it were, to you,
We, Thunder-wielding Indra!
Count ourselves as trees rejected, And unfit to burn.

अमन्महीदनाशवोऽनुग्रासश्च वृत्रहन्।
सकृत्सु ते महता शूर राधसानु स्तोमं मुदीमहि॥१४॥

O Vṛtra-slayer! We were thought slow,
And unready for the fight.
Yet once in your great bounty,
May we have delight, O Hero, after praising you.

यदि स्तोमं मम श्रवदस्माकमिन्द्रमिन्दवः।
तिरः पवित्रं ससृवांस आशवो मन्दन्तु तुग्र्यावृधः॥१५॥

If he will listen to my laud,
Then may our Soma-drops that flow
Rapidly through the strainer gladden Indra!
Drops due to the Tugryas' Strengthener.

आ त्व१द्य सधस्तुतिं वावातुः सख्युरा गहि।
उपस्तुतिर्मघोनां प्र त्वावत्वधा ते वश्मि सुष्टुतिम्॥१६॥

Come now unto the common laud of you
And of your faithful friend.
So may our wealthy nobles' praise
Give joy to you. Fain would I sing your eulogy.

सोता हि सोममद्रिभिरेमेनमप्सु धावत।
गव्या वस्त्रेव वासयन्त इन्नरो निर्धुक्षन्वक्षणाभ्यः॥१७॥

Press out the Soma with the stones,
And in the waters wash it clean.

The men investing it with raiment made of milk,
Shall milk it forth from out the stems.

अध ज्मो अध वा दिवो बृहतो रोचनादधि।
अया वर्धस्व तन्वा गिरा ममा जाता सुक्रतो पृण॥१८॥

Whether you come from earth,
Or from the lustre of the lofty heaven.
Wax stronger in your body
Through my song of praise,
Fill full all creatures, O Most Wise!

इन्द्राय सु मदिन्तमं सोमं सोता वरेण्यम्।
शक्र एणं पीपयद्विश्वया धिया हिन्वानं न वाजयुम्॥१९॥

For Indra press the Soma out,
Most gladdening and most excellent.
May Śakra make it swell
Sent forth with every prayer and asking,
As it were for strength.

मा त्वा सोमस्य गल्दया सदा याचन्नहं गिरा।
भूर्णिं मृगं न सवनेषु चुक्रुधं क ईशानं न याचिषत्॥२०॥

Let me not, still beseeching you
With earnest song at Soma rites,
Anger you like some wild beast,
Who would not beseech him,
Who has power to grant his prayer?

मदेनेषितं मदमुग्रमुग्रेण शवसा।
विश्वेषां तरुतारं मदच्युतं मदे हि ष्मा ददाति नः॥२१॥

The draught made swift with rapturous joy,
Effectual with its mighty strength.
All-conquering distilling transport,
Let him drink, for he in ecstasy gives us gifts.

शेवारे वार्या पुरु देवो मर्ताय दाशुषे।
स सुन्वते च स्तुवते च रासते विश्वगूर्तो अरिष्टुतः।।२२।।

Where bliss is not, may He, All-praised God,
Whom the pious glorify,
Bestow great wealth upon the mortal worshipper,
Who sheds the juice and praises him.

एन्द्र याहि मत्स्व चित्रेण देव राधसा।
सरो न प्रास्युदरं सपीतिभिरा सोमोभिरुरु स्फिरम्।।२३।।

Come Indra! And rejoice yourself,
O God, in manifold affluence,
You fill like a lake your vast capacious bulk
With Soma and with draughts besides.

आ त्वा सहस्रमा शतं युक्ता रथे हिरण्यये।
ब्रह्मयुजो हरय इन्द्र केशिनो वहन्तु सोमपीतये।।२४।।

A thousand and a hundred Steeds
Are harnessed to your golden car.
So may the long-maned Bays,
Yoked by devotion,
Bring Indra to drink the Soma juice.

आ त्वा रथे हिरण्यये हरी मयूरशेप्या।
शितिपृष्ठा वहतां मध्वो अन्धसो विवक्षणस्य पीतये।।२५।।

Yoked to your chariot wrought of gold,
May your two Bays with peacock tails,
Convey you here, Steeds with their white backs,
To drink sweet juice that makes us eloquent.

पिबा त्व१स्य गिर्वणः सुतस्य पूर्वपा इव।
परिष्कृतस्य रसिन इयमासुतिश्चारुर्मदाय पत्यते।।२६।।

So drink, You Lover of the Song,
As the first drinker of this juice,
This the outpouring of the savoury sap prepared
Is good and meet to gladden you.

य एको अस्ति दंसना महाँ उग्रो अभि व्रतैः।
गमत्स शिप्री न स योषदा गमद्धवं न परि वर्जति।।२७।।

He who alone by wondrous deed is Mighty,
Strong by holy works.
May he come, fair of cheek, may he not stay afar,
But come and turn not from our call.

त्वं पुरं चरिष्ण्वं वधैः शुष्णस्य सं पिणक्।
त्वं भा अनु चरो अध द्विता यदिन्द्र हव्यो भुवः।।२८।।

Śuṣṇa's quick moving castle,
You have crushed to pieces with your bolts.
You, Indra! from of old, has followed after light,
Since we have had you to invoke.

मम त्वा सूर उदिते मम मध्यंदिने दिवः।
मम प्रपित्वे अपिशर्वरे वसवा स्तोमासो अवृत्सत।।२९।।

My praises when the Sun has risen,
My praises at the time of noon,
My praises at the coming of the gloom of night,
O Vasu! have gone forth to you.

स्तुहि स्तुहीदेते घा ते मंहिष्ठासो मघोनाम्।
निन्दिताश्वः प्रपथी परमज्या मघस्य मेध्यातिथे!।।३०।।

Praise, yes, praise him.
Of princes, these are the most liberal of their gifts.
These, Paramajyā, Ninditāśva, Prapathī,
Most bounteous, O Medhyātithi!

आ यदश्वान्वनन्वतः श्रद्धयाहं रथे रुहम्।
उत वामस्य वसुनश्चिकेतति यो अस्ति याद्वः पशुः।।३१।।

When to the car, by faith,
I yoked the horses longing for the way,
For skilled is Yadu's son in dealing precious wealth,
he who is rich in herds of kine.

य ऋज्रा मह्यं मामहे सह त्वचा हिरण्यया।
एष विश्वान्यभ्यस्तु सौभगासङ्गस्य स्वनद्रथः।।३२।।

May he who gave me two brown steeds,
Together with their clothes of gold.
May he, Āsaṅga's son Svanadratha,
Obtain all joy and high felicities.

अध प्लायोगिरति दासदन्यानासङ्गो अग्ने दशभिः सहस्रैः।
अधोक्षणो दश मह्यं रुशन्तो नळा इव सरसो निरतिष्ठन्।।३३।।

Plāyoga's son Āsaṅga, by ten thousand,
O Agni! has surpassed the rest in giving,
For me ten bright-hued oxen have come forward
Like lotus stalks from out a lake upstanding.

अन्वस्य स्थूरं ददृशे पुरस्तादनस्थ ऊरुरवरम्बमाणः।
शश्वती नार्यभिचक्ष्याह सुभद्रमर्य भोजनं बिभर्षि।।३४।।

When her husband's perfect restoration
to his lost strength and manhood was apparent,
His consort Śāsvatī with joy addressed him —
"Now are you well, my lord! and shall be happy".

Part III
Who Praised the Self

17

Sārparājñī

SĀRPARĀJÑĪ is the seer of *R̥V* X.189, containing three *mantras*. Since it is addressed to Sārparājñī or Sūryā, this is treated as an *ātmastuti*. Thus, Sārparājñī is the R̥ṣikā as well as the Devatā for this *sūktam*. *Br̥haddevatā* has included her name in the list of R̥ṣikās — *śrirlākṣā sarparājñī vāk*[1] — as well as in the list of Devatās — *āyaṁ gauriti yat-sūktaṁ sārparājñī svayaṁ jagau.*[2] Ācārya Sāyaṇa also has confirmed her as a R̥ṣikā as well as a Devatā — *sārparājñī nāmar̥ṣikā, saiva devatā sūryo veti.*[3]

Interestingly, these three *mantras* have been repeated in the other three Vedas — *Yajurveda* III.6-8 (addressed to Agni), *Sāmaveda* 630-632, again *Sāmaveda* 1376-1378 (addressed to Sūryā or Ātmā in both the places) and *Atharvaveda* VI.31.1-3 (addressed to Gau, however credited to Uparivrabhava) XX.48.4-6 (addressed to Gau, Sūrya).

R̥V X.189 (3 mantras)

ऋषिका - सार्पराज्ञी। देवता - सार्पराज्ञी सूर्या वा। छन्द - गायत्री।

R̥ṣikā — Sārparājñī, Devatā — Sārparājñī or Sūryā
Metre — Gāyatrī

---

1. *Br̥had.,* II.84.
2. *Br̥had.,* VIII.89.
3. *R̥V.Sā.Bh.,* X.189.

आयं गौ पृश्निरक्रमीदसदन्मातरं पुरः।
पितरं च प्रयन्त्स्वः॥१॥[4]

This spotted Bull has come,
And sat before the Mother in the east.
Advancing to his Father heaven.

अन्तश्चरति रोचनास्य प्राणादपानती।
व्यख्यन्महिषो दिवम्॥२॥

Expiring when he draws his breath,
She moves along the lucid spheres,
The Bull shines out through all the sky.

त्रिंशद्धाम वि राजति वाक्पतङ्गाय धीयते।
प्रति वस्तोरह द्युभिः॥३॥

Song is bestowed upon the Bird,
It rules supreme through thirty realms,
Throughout the days at break of morn.

4. This *mantra* of *R̥V* X.189.1 with some variation is part of the Navagraha-Sūktam, addressed to Rāhu.

18

Vāgāmbhṛṇī

VĀGĀMBHṚṆĪ is the seer of *ṚV* X.125, containing eight *mantras*. It is known as Devī-Sūktam or Vāk-Sūktam. This is a self-laudatory hymn — *ātmastuti*; hence, she is the Ṛṣikā as well as the Devatā. Vāgāmbhṛṇī is the daughter of Ṛṣi Ambhṛṇa. After her vision (*brahma-sākṣātkāra*) she identifies herself with Devi. Bṛhaddevatākāra makes a brief mention of this *sūkta* — *ahaṁ vāk-sūktam.*[1] Devi-sūktam is conventionally chanted in *Durgāsapataśatī* (containing 700 *ślokas*) *Caṇḍī*. The eight *mantras* clearly establish the vision of Advaita Vedānta.

ṚV X.125 (8 mantras)
(Devī-Sūktam or Vāk-Sūktam)
ऋषिका – वागाम्भृणी। देवता – वागाम्भृणी (आत्मस्तुति)।
छन्द – त्रिष्टुप्, २ जगती।

Ṛṣikā — Vāgāmbhṛṇī, Devatā — Vāgāmbhṛṇī
Metre — Triṣṭup, 2 Jagatī

अहं रुद्रेभिर्वसुभिश्चराम्यहमादित्यैरुत विश्वदेवैः।
अहं मित्रावरुणोभा बिभर्म्यहमिन्द्राग्नी अहमश्विनोभा।।१।।

I travel with the Rudras and the Vasus,
With the Ādityas and All-Gods I wander.
I hold aloft both Varuṇa and Mitra,
Indra and Agni, and the Pair of Aśvins.

1. *Bṛhad.*, VIII.43.

अहं सोममाहनसं बिभर्म्यहं त्वष्टारमुत पूषणं भगम्।
अहं दधामि द्रविणं हविष्मते सुप्राव्ये३ यजमानाय सुन्वते।।२।।

I cherish and sustain high-swelling Soma,
And Tvaṣṭā I support, Pūṣan, and Bhaga.
I load with wealth the zealous sacrificer
Who pours the juice and offers his oblation.

अहं राष्ट्री सङ्गमनी वसूनां चिकितुषी प्रथमा यज्ञियानाम्।
तां मा देवा व्यदधुः पुरुत्रा भूरिस्थात्रां भूर्यावेशयन्तीम्।।३।।

I am the Queen,
The gatherer-up of treasures, most thoughtful,
First of those who merit worship.
Thus Gods have established me in many places,
With many homes to enter and abide in.

मया सो अन्नमत्ति यो विपश्यति यः प्राणिति य ईं शृणोत्युक्तम्।
अमन्तवो मां त उप क्षियन्ति श्रुधि श्रुत श्रद्धिवं ते वदामि।।४।।

Through me alone
All eat the food that feeds them,
Each man who sees, breathes,
Hears the word outspoken.
They know it not, but yet they dwell beside me.
Hear, one and all! The truth as I declare it.

अहमेव स्वयमिदं वदामि जुष्टं देवेभिरुत मानुषेभिः।
यं कामये तं तमुग्रं कृणोमि तं ब्रह्माणं तमृषिं तं सुमेधाम्।।५।।

I, verily, myself announce and utter the word
That Gods and men alike shall welcome.
I make the man I love exceedingly mighty,
Make him a sage, Ṛṣi, and a Brahmā.

अहं रुद्राय धनुरा तनोमि ब्रह्मद्विषे शरवे हन्तवा उ।
अहं जनाय समदं कृणोम्यहं द्यावापृथिवी आ विवेश॥६॥

I bind the bow for Rudra that his arrow may
strike and slay the hater of devotion.
I rouse and order battle for the people,
And I have penetrated Earth and Heaven.

अहं सुवे पितरमस्य मूर्धन्मम योनिरप्स्व१न्तः समुद्रे।
ततो वि तिष्ठे भुवनानु विश्वोतामूं द्यां वर्ष्मणोप स्पृशामि॥७॥

On the world's summit I bring forth the father,
My home is in the waters, in the ocean.
From there I extend o'er all existing creatures,
And touch even the heaven with my forehead.

अहमेव वात इव प्र वाम्यारभमाणा भुवनानि विश्वा।
परो दिवा पर एना पृथिव्यैतावती महिना सं बभूव॥८॥

I breathe a strong breath
Like the wind and tempest,
While I hold together all existence.
Beyond this wide earth and beyond the heavens
I have become so mighty in my grandeur.

19

Śraddhā Kāmāyanī

Śraddhā Kāmāyanī is the seer of *R̥V* X.151, containing five *mantra*s addressed to Śraddhā, which is known as Śraddhā-Sūktam. The *sūktam* praises the attitude of Śraddhā[1] of the giver and requests Śraddhā (Devatā/Devī) to bless the giver. The title Kāmāyanī (*gotra-apatya*) is added after her name since she belongs to Kāma *gotra*. Br̥haddevatākāra has presented her as a R̥ṣikā[2] as well as the Devatā.[3] She is presented as the daughter of Sūrya in the Brāhmaṇa texts — *śraddhā vai sūryasya duhitā'*,[4] and as *prajāpati-duhitā* in *Tai.Br.* II.3.10.1. Ācārya Sāyaṇa has presented her as a *R̥ṣikā* — *śraddhayā iti pañcarcaṁ trayoviṁsaṁ sūktamānuṣṭubhaṁ śraddhādevatyaṁ, kāmagotrajā śraddhānāmarṣikā*.[5]

R̥V X.151 (5 mantras) (Śraddhā-Sūktam)
ऋषिका – श्रद्धा कामायनी। देवता – श्रद्धा। छन्द – अनुष्टुप्।
R̥ṣikā — Śraddhā Kāmāyanī, Devatā — Śraddhā
Metre — Anuṣṭup

श्रद्धयाग्निः समिध्यते श्रद्धया हूयते हविः।
श्रद्धां भगस्य मूर्धनि वचसा वेदयामसि।।१।।

---

1. Śraddhā does not have an exact English translation, since such a concept is not there. "Faith" is the nearest term.
2. *Br̥had.*, II.84.
3. *Br̥had.*, II.74.
4. *Śa.Br̥.*, XII.7.3.11.
5. *R̥V.Sā.Bh.*, X.151.

By Faith is Agni kindled,
Through Faith is oblation offered up.
We celebrate with praises Faith
Upon the height of happiness.

प्रियं श्रद्धे ददतः प्रियं श्रद्धे दिदासतः।
प्रियं भोजेषु यज्वस्विदं म उदितं कृधि।।२।।

Bless you the man who gives, O Faith!
Faith, bless the man who would give happily.
Bless you the liberal worshippers:
Bless you the word that I have said

यथा देवा असुरेषु श्रद्धामुग्रेषु चक्रिरे।
एवं भोजेषु यज्वस्वस्माकमुदितं कृधि।।३।।

Even as the Deities maintained faith in the mighty
Asuras, So make this uttered wish of mine true
For the liberal worshippers.

श्रद्धां देवा यजमाना वायुगोपा उपासते।
श्रद्धां हृदय्य१याकूत्या श्रद्धया विन्दते वसु।।४।।

Guarded by Vāyu, Gods and men who sacrifice
draw near to Faith.
Man wins Faith by yearnings of the heart,
And opulence by Faith.

श्रद्धां प्रातर्हवामहे श्रद्धां मध्यन्दिनं परि।
श्रद्धां सूर्यस्य निम्रुचि श्रद्धे श्रद्धापयेह नः।।५।।

Faith in the early morning,
Faith at noonday will we invocate,
Faith at the setting of the Sun.
O Faith! Endow us with belief.

20

Dakṣiṇā Prājāpatyā

Dakṣiṇā Prājāpatyā is the seer of the *sūktam R̥V* X.107, containing eleven *mantra*s addressed the *yajamāna*s — the giver of honorarium or sacrificial fees. This *sūkta* is alternatively attributed to Divya Āṅgirasa. Being the daughter of the Prajāpati, she gets the title Prājāpatyā (*apatya-vācaka*). As per a Purāṇic story, Dakṣiṇā is the sister of Prajāpati and the mother of twelve Yamadevas.

Br̥haddevatā explains this *sūkta* as praising her own self, or the liberal and charitable people gifting the sacrificial fees.[1] Acārya Sāyaṇa presents her seerhood as — *prajāpateḥ sutā dakṣiṇā, sā vā r̥ṣikā.*[2]

R̥V X.107 (11 mantras)

ऋषि – दिव्य आङ्गिरसः, दक्षिणा प्राजापत्या (ऋषिका) वा।
देवता – दक्षिणा, दक्षिणादातारो वा। छन्द – त्रिष्टुप्।

R̥ṣi — Divya Āṅgirasa /or Dakṣiṇā Prājāpatyā (R̥ṣikā)
Devatā — Dakṣiṇā Metre — Triṣṭup

आविरभून्महि माघोनमेषां विश्वं जीवं तमसो निरमोचि।
महि ज्योतिः पितृभिर्दत्तमागादुरुः पन्था दक्षिणाया अदर्शि॥१॥

These men's great bounty has been manifested,
And the whole world of life set free from darkness.

1. *Br̥had.*, VIII.22-23.
2. *R̥V.Sā.Bh.*, X.107.

Great light has come vouchsafed us by the Fathers,
Apparent is the spacious path of Gift.

उच्चा दिवि दक्षिणावन्तो अस्थुर्ये अश्वदाः सह ते सूर्येण।
हिरण्यदा अमृतत्वं भजन्ते वासोदाः सोम प्र तिरन्त आयुः।।२।।

High up in heaven abide the Gift-givers;
They who give steeds dwell with the Sun forever,
They who give gold are blessed with life eternal,
They who give robes prolong their lives, O Soma!

दैवी पूर्तिर्दक्षिणा देवयज्या न कवारिभ्यो नहि ते पृणन्ति।
अथा नरः प्रयतदक्षिणासोऽवद्यभिया बहवः पृणन्ति।।३।।

Not from the misers — for they give not freely,
Comes Gift at sacrifice, God's satisfaction,
Yes, many men with hands stretched out with Gift,
Present their gifts because they dread dishonour.

शतधारं वायुमर्कं स्वर्विदं नृचक्षसस्ते अभि चक्षते हविः।
ये पृणन्ति प्र च यच्छन्ति संगमे ते दक्षिणां दुहते सप्तमातरम्।।४।।

These who observe mankind regard oblation
As streamy Vāyu and light-finding Arka.
They satisfy and give their gifts in assembly,
And pour in streams, The seven-mothered Gift.

दक्षिणावान् प्रथमो हूत एति दक्षिणावान् ग्रामणीरग्रमेति।
तमेव मन्ये नृपतिं जनानां यः प्रथमो दक्षिणामाविवाय।।५।।

He who brings Gift comes as first invited,
Chief of the hamlet comes the Gift-bearer.
Him I account the ruler of the people,
Who was the first to introduce the Gift.

तमेव ऋषिं तमु ब्रह्माणमाहुर्यज्ञन्यं सामगामुक्थशासम्।
स शुक्रस्य तन्वो वेद तिस्रो यः प्रथमो दक्षिणया रराध॥६॥

They call him Ṛṣi, Brahmā, Sāma-chanter,
reciter of the laud, leader of worship.
The brightly shining God's three forms he knows,
Who first bestowed the sacrificial Gift.

दक्षिणाश्वं दक्षिणा गां ददाति दक्षिणा चन्द्रमुत यद्धिरण्यम्।
दक्षिणान्नं वनुते यो न आत्मा दक्षिणां वर्म कृणुते विजानन्॥७॥

Gift bestows the horses, bestows the bullocks,
Gift bestows, moreover gold that glisters.
Gift gives food, which is our life and spirit,
He who is wise takes Gift for his armour.

न भोजा मम्रुर्न न्यर्थमीयुर्न रिष्यन्ति न व्यथन्ते ह भोजाः।
इदं यद्विश्वं भुवनं स्वश्चैतत्सर्वं दक्षिणैभ्यो ददाति॥८॥

The liberal die not, never are they ruined,
The liberal suffer neither harm not trouble.
The light of heaven, the universe about us,
All this does sacrificial Gift gives them.

भोजा जिग्युः सुरभिं योनिमग्रे भोजा जिग्युर्वध्वं१ या सुवासाः।
भोजा जिग्युरन्तः पेयं सुराया भोजा जिग्युर्ये अहूताः प्रयन्ति॥९॥

First have the liberal gained a fragrant dwelling,
And got themselves a bride in fair apparel.
The liberal have obtained their draught of liquor,
And conquered those,
Who, unprovoked, assailed them.

भोजायाश्वं सं मृजन्त्याशुं भोजायास्ते कन्या३ शुम्भमाना।
भोजस्येदं पुष्करिणीव वेश्म परिष्कृतं देवामानेव चित्रम्॥१०॥

They deck the fleet steed for the bounteous giver,
The maiden adorns herself and waits to meet him.
His home is like a lake with lotus-blossoms,
Like the God's palaces adorned and splendid.

भोजमश्वाः सुष्ठुवाहो वहन्ति सुवृद्रथो वर्तते दक्षिणायाः
भोजं देवासोऽवता भरेषु भोजः शत्रून्त्समनीकेषु जेता।।११।।

Steeds good at draught convey the liberal giver,
And lightly rolling moves the car of Gift.
Assist, you Gods, the liberal man in battles,
The liberal giver conquers foes in combat.

21

Rātri-Bhāradvājī

Rātri-Bhāradvājī is the alternative seer of *R̥V* X.127 containing eight *r̥cā*. This *sūktam* is addressed to Rātri, so she is the Devatā.

She is the sister of Uṣas, and like her is called a daughter of heaven. She is not conceived as the dark, but as the bright starlit night. Decked with all splendour, she drives away the darkness. At her approach, men, animals, and birds go to rest. She protects her worshippers from the wolf and the thief, guiding them to safety. Under the name Nākta, combined with Uṣas, Night appears as a dual divinity with Dawn in the form of Uṣāsā-nāktā[1] and Nāktoṣāsā,[2] occurring in twenty scattered *mantras* in the *R̥gveda*.[3]

Incidentally, this *sūktam* titled Rātri-Sūktam, is conventionally chanted in *Durgā-sapataśati* (containing 700 *ślokas*) *Caṇḍī*. Being the daughter of R̥ṣi Bharadvāja, she has the title Bhāradvājī (*apatyārthe*). Br̥haddevatākāra has accepted Rātri as the Devatā of the *sūktam*.[4] Ācārya Sāyaṇa has presented her as *bhāradvāja-sutā — bharadvājasya sutā rātryākhyā asya sūktasyar̥ṣikā, gāyatraṁ rātridevatākam*.[5]

Rātri-Bhāradvājī is also the seer of *YV* XXXIV.32. She is known

---

1. *R̥V* I.13.7 (Āprī-Sūktam); VII.2.69 (Āprī-Sūktam).
2. *R̥V* I.142.7 (Āprī-Sūktam).
3. Cf. A.A. Macdonell, *A Vedic Reader for Students*, p. 203.
4. *Br̥had.*, VIII.44.
5. *R̥V.Sā.Bh.*, X.127.

as Kaśipā Bharadvāja-duhitā in this. This single *mantra* is addressed to Rātri.

ṚV X.127 (8 mantras)
(Rātri-Sūktam)
ऋषि – कुशिकः सौभरः, रात्रि भारद्वाजी (ऋषिका) वा।
देवता – रात्रिः। छन्द – गायत्री।

Ṛṣi — Kuśika Saubhara or Rātri-Bhāradvājī (Ṛṣikā)
Devatā — Rātri; Metre — Gāyatrī

रात्री व्यख्यदायती पुरुत्रा देव्य१ क्षभिः।
विश्वा अधि श्रियोऽधित॥१॥

Night approaching has looked forth in many
places with her eyes,
she has put on all glories.

ओर्वप्रा अमर्त्या निवतो देव्यु१द्वतः।
ज्योतिषा बाधते तमः॥२॥

The Immortal Goddess has pervaded the wide space,
the depths, and the heights,
With light she drives away the darkness.

निरु स्वसारमस्कृतोषसं देव्यायती।
अपेदु हासते तमः॥३॥

The Goddess approaching has turned out
her sister Dawn;
Away too will go the darkness.

सा नो अद्य यस्या वयं नि ते यामन्नविक्ष्महि।
वृक्षे न वसतिं वयः॥४॥

So to us today you (have approached),
At whose approach we have come home,
As birds to their nest upon the tree.

नि ग्रामासो अविक्षत नि पद्वन्तो नि पक्षिणः।
नि श्येनासश्चिदर्थिनः।।५।।

Home have gone the villagers,
Home creatures with feet,
Home those with wings,
Home even the falcons.

यावया वृक्यं१ वृकं यवय स्तेनमूर्म्ये।
अथा नः सुतरा भव।।६।।

Ward off the she-wolf and the wolf,
Ward off the thief, O Night!
Be easy for us to pass.

उप मा पेपिशत्तमः कृष्णं व्यक्तमस्थित।
उष ऋणेव यातय।।७।।

The darkness thickly painting,
Black, palpable, has approached me,
O Dawn! Clear it like debts.

उप ते गा इवाकरं वृणीष्व दुहितर्दिवः।
रात्रि स्तोमं न जिग्युषे।।८।।

Like kine I have delivered up to you a hymn,
Choose it O Daughter of Heaven!
O Night! Like a song of praise to a victor.

22

Sūryā-Sāvitrī

Sūryā-Sāvitrī (daughter of Sūrya) is the seer of *R̥V* X.85 containing 47 *r̥cā*, conventionally used in the weddings. She is the daughter of Savitā (Lord Sun), hence the title Sāvitrī (*apatyārthe*). This *sūktam* contains the complete description of her wedding ritual. Hence, this is known as Sūryā-Sūktam or Vivāha-Sūktam. Incidentally, Uṣā, the daughter of Sūrya, is also known as Sūryā. *R̥V* VI.58.4 refers to Sūryā as the sister of Pūṣā. In the Brāhmaṇa texts, Sūryā-Sāvitrī is presented as the daughter of Prajāpati — *prajāpatir-vai-somāya rājñe duhitaraṁ prāyacchat sūryāṁ sāvitrim.*[1] She has also been presented as the wife of Soma or the Aśvins. In X.85.8 clearly the bridegrooms were the Aśvins. And X.85.9 says both Soma and the Aśvins were her wooers, but Sūrya, the father, gave her way to the Aśvins. Br̥haddevatākāra has presented her in three forms of Uṣas — Sāvitrī, Sūryā and Vr̥ṣākapāyi. She is Uṣas before sunrise, Sūryā during noon, and at sunset she goes down as Vr̥ṣākapāyi.[2] Ācārya Sāyaṇa has presented her as Savitā-sutā — *tatra satyena iti saptacatvāriṁ śadr̥cāṁ prathamaṁ sūktaṁ savitr̥sutāyāḥ sūryāyā ārṣam.*[3]

Interestingly, of the 47 *mantra*s of this Vivāha-Sūktam, at least 42 are repeated *in toto*, or with some changes, and in a different sequence in the fourteenth (31 *mantra*s repeated) and fifteenth (11 *mantra*s repeated) *kāṇḍa*s of the *Atharvaveda*

1. *Ai.Br.*, IV.7.
2. *Br̥had.*, VII.119 and 121.
3. *R̥V.Sā.Bh.*, X.85.

Vedic Wedding being performed chanting Sūryā-Sāvitrī-Sūktam

credited to Sūryā-Sāvitrī. Both the *kāṇḍa*s are about her/Vedic wedding, the seer also being Sūryā-Sāvitrī.

*Mantra*s X.18 and 19, with minor modifications, are also repeated in the *Atharvaveda* as *AV* VII.86.1 and 2, the Ṛṣi being Atharvā, and the Devatās being Sāvitrī, Sūrya and Candramā.

ṚV X.85 (47 mantras)

ऋषि – सूर्या सावित्री (ऋषिका)

देवता – १-५ सोमः ६-१६ सूर्याविवाहः, १७ देवाः, १८ सोमार्कौ, १९ चन्द्रमाः,. २०-२८ विवाहमन्त्राआशीर्वादाः, २९-३० वधूवासः संस्पर्शनिन्दा, ३१ दम्पती-यक्ष्मनाशनम्, ३२-४७ सूर्यासावित्री।

छन्द – अनुष्टुप्; १४, १९-२१, २३-२४, २६, ३६-३७, ४४; त्रिष्टुप्; १८, २७, ४३ जगती; ३४ उरोबृहती।

(Sūryā-Sūktam or Vivāha-Sūktam)

Ṛṣikā — Sūryā-Sāvitrī

Devatā — 1-5 Soma, 6-16 Sūryā Vivāha, 17 Devagaṇa, 18 - Soma and Arka, 19 Candramā, 20-28 Wedding mantras and Blessings, 29-30 - Bride's Garment 31 Wedding Couple & Yakṣma-nāśana, 32-47 Sūryā-Sāvitrī

Metre — Anuṣṭup; 14, 19-21, 23-24, 26, 36-37, 44 Triṣṭup; 18, 27, 43 Jagatī; 34 Urobṛhatī

सत्येनोत्तभिता भूमिः सूर्येणोत्तभिता द्यौः।
ऋतेनादित्यास्तिष्ठन्ति दिवि सोमो अधि श्रितः॥१॥

By Truth is the earth established;
by the Sun are the heavens sustained;
by righteousness the Ādityas stand secure;
Soma holds his place in the heaven.

सोमेनादित्या बलिनः सोमेन पृथिवी मही।
अथो नक्षत्राणामेषामुपस्थे सोम आहितः॥२॥

By Soma are the Ādityas strong,
By Soma mighty is the earth.
Thus, Soma in the midst of all these
constellations has his place.

सोमं मन्यते पपिवान् यत्संपिंषन्त्योषधिम्।
सोमं यं ब्रह्माणो विदुर्न तस्याश्नाति कश्चन॥३॥

One thinks himself that he has drunk the Soma's juice;
when they crush up the herb;
What the Wise truly know as Soma,
Of that no human-being partakes.

आच्छद्विधानैर्गुपितो बार्हतैः सोम रक्षितः।
ग्राव्णामिच्छृण्वन् तिष्ठसि न ते अश्नाति पार्थिवः॥४॥

O Soma! Guarded sheltering rules,
Defended by watchmen (or hymns in Bṛhatī),
You stand listening to the pressing-stones,
No earthly man tastes you.

यत्त्वा देव प्रपिबन्ति तत आ प्यायसे पुनः।
वायुः सोमस्य रक्षिता समानां मास आकृतिः॥५॥

O Soma! When they drink you,
Then, You swell up again.
Vāyu is Soma's defender,
As the Moon is that shapes the years.

रैभ्यासीदनुदेयी नाराशंसी न्योचनी।
सूर्याया भद्रमिद्वासो गाथयैति परिष्कृतम्॥६॥

The Raibhī was the parting (song),
And Nārāśaṁsī was the welcoming (song) one.

Lovely indeed was Sūryā's robe,
She goes adorned with song (Gāthā).

चित्तिरा उपबर्हणं चक्षुरा अभ्यञ्जनम्।
द्यौर्भूमिः कोश आसीद्यदयात्सूर्या पतिम्।।७।।

Thought was the pillow of her couch,
Sight was the ointment of her eyes.
Heaven and earth were her coffer,
When Sūryā went unto her husband.

स्तोमा आसन्प्रतिधयः कुरीरं छन्द ओपशः।
सूर्याया अश्विना वराग्निरासीत्पुरोगवः।।८।।

Laudatory hymns were the cross-bars
(of the chariot-pole),
Kurīra (a Vedic metre) decked in her head-dress,
The bridegrooms were the Aśvins,
Agni was the forerunner.

सोमो वधूयुरभवदश्विनास्तामुभा वरा।
सूर्यां यत्पत्ये शंसन्तीं मनसा सविताददात्।।९।।

Soma was once her wooer,
So were both Aśvins,
Who became the bridegrooms,
When the Sun-God Savitar
Gave away the willing Sūryā unto them.

मनो अस्या अन आसीद् द्यौरासीदुत च्छदिः।
शुक्रावनड्वाहावास्तां यदयात्सूर्या गृहम्।।१०।।

Her mind was the bridal chariot,
Heaven was the canopy,
Bright were both Steers (or Sun and Moon?)

that drew it,
When Sūryā went to her husband's home.

ऋक्सामाभ्यामभिहितौ गावौ ते सामनावितः।
श्रोत्रं ते चक्रे आस्तां दिवि पन्थाश्चराचरः॥११॥

Your Steers were steady/in place,
haltered with the holy verse (*ṛk*) and chant (*sāman*),
All ears were your (two) chariot wheels:
Your wandering tracks in the sky.

शुची ते चक्रे यात्या व्यानो अक्ष आहतः।
अनो मनस्मयं सूर्यारोहत्प्रयती पतिम्॥१२॥

Pure were your wheels, as you went,
Wind was the axle fastened there.
Mounted on the chariot of mind,
Sūryā, proceeded to her husband.

सूर्याया वहतुः प्रागात्सविता यमवासृजत्।
अघासु हन्यन्ते गावोऽर्जुन्योः पर्युह्यते॥१३॥

The bridal pomp (dowry?) of Sūryā,
Which Savitar sent off, has moved along.
In Maghā constellation are oxen slain,
in Arjunis (Pūrvā and Uttarā-Phālgunis[4])
they send the bride (to her husband's home).

यदश्विना पृच्छमानावयातं त्रिचक्रेणं वहतुं सूर्यायाः।
विश्वे देवा अनु तद्वामजानन् पुत्रः पितरावववृणीत पूषा॥१४॥

O Aśvins! When on your three-wheeled,
You came as wooers unto Sūryā's bridal.

4. The moon in the constellation Maghā (the Sickle in the Leo), moves to Pūrvā-Phālgunī (Leonis) next day, and Uttarā-Phālgunī the day after.

Then all the gods agreed to your proposal,
Pūṣan as son chose you as Fathers.

यदयातं शुभस्पती वरेयं सूर्यामुप।
क्वैकं चक्रं वामासीत्क्व देष्ट्राय तस्थथुः॥१५॥

O You Two Lords of lustre!
When you came to Sūryā's wooing,
Where was one chariot-wheel of yours?
Where stood you for the Sire's command?

द्वे ते चक्रे सूर्ये ब्रह्माण ऋतुथा विदुः।
अथैकं चक्रं यद्गुहा तदद्धातय इद्विदुः॥१६॥

O Sūryā! Those two wheels of yours,
The Wise know as the seasons.
The third one, that is a secret,
Only the Wise know.

सूर्यायै देवेभ्यो मित्राय वरुणाय च।
ये भूतस्य प्रचेतस इदं तेभ्योऽकरं नमः॥१७॥

Unto Sūryā and the gods,
Unto Mitra and to Varuṇa
Unto them who are thoughtful well-wishers of all
I pay this homage.

पूर्वापरं चरतो माययैतौ शिशू क्रीळन्तौ परि यातो अध्वरम्।
विश्वान्यन्यो भुवनाभिचष्ट ऋतूँरन्यो विदधज्जायते पुनः॥१८॥

These two young ones (the Sun and the Moon)
move from east to west by their splendour,
Sporting they reach the ocean/sacrifice.
One of the pair (the Sun) beholds all beings,

The other (the Moon) orders seasons,[5]
and is born again.[6]

नवोनवो भवति जायमानोऽह्नां केतुरुषसामेत्यग्रम्।
भागं देवेभ्यो वि दधात्यायन् प्र चन्द्रमास्तिरते दीर्घमायुः।।१९।।

Ever new are you (O Moon!), being born everyday,
Sign (Ketu) of the days you are.
O Sun! You go to the apex of the dawn,
and dispose for the gods their portion.
O Moon! You prolong the days of our existence.

सुकिंशुकं शल्मलिं विश्वरूपं हिरण्यवर्णं सुवृतं सुचक्रम्।
आ रोह सूर्ये अमृतस्य लोकं स्योनं पत्ये वहतुं कृणुष्व।।२०।।

Mount this, well-shaped, well-wheeled,
light-rolling, golden-hued chariot,
well-flowered with Kinśuka and Śalmali.
O Sūryā! Make the bridal-chariot to the immortal world,
pleasant to the husbands.

उदीर्ष्वातः पतिवती ह्येषा विश्वावसुं नमसा गीर्भिरीळे।
अन्यामिच्छ पितृषदं व्यक्तां स ते भागो जनुषा तस्य विद्धि।।२१।।

Rise up from here, O Viśvāvasu!
With homage do we praise you
Seek in her father's home another fair one,
That is your portion by right of birth,
Know that well.

उदीर्ष्वातो विश्वावसो नमसेळामहे त्वा।
अन्यामिच्छ प्रफर्व्यं१सं जायां पत्या सृज।।२२।।

---

5. I would think the Sun causes the seasons.
6. The Moon is born again since it waxes and wanes.

Rise up from hence, O Viśvāvasu!
With reverence, we worship you.
Seek you another willing maiden,
And with her husband leave the bride.

अनृक्षरा: ऋजव: सन्तु पन्था येभि: सखायो यन्ति नो वरेयम्।
समर्यमा सं भगो नो निनीयात्सं जास्पत्यं सुयममस्तु देवा:।।२३।।

Let the path be thornless, straight in direction,
Whereon our friends travel a-wooing to us.
Together with Aryaman and Bhaga lead us,
May the union of the couple be perfect.

प्र त्वा मुञ्चामि वरुणस्य पाशाद्येन त्वाबध्नात्सविता सुशेव:।
ऋतस्य योनौ सुकृतस्य लोकेऽरिष्टां त्वा सह पत्या दधामि।।२४।।

I release you from Varuṇa's fetter,
With which the propitious Savitar bound you,
To the world of virtuous action,
I send you uninjured with your consort.

प्रेतो मुञ्चामि नामुत: सुबद्धाममुतस्करम्।
यथेयमिन्द्र मीढ्व: सुपुत्रा सुभगासति।।२५।।

Hence, and not thence, I send you free.
I make you softly fettered there,
That, Bounteous Indra, She may live,
Blessed with her husband and children.

पूषा त्वेतो नयतु हस्तगृह्याश्विना त्वा प्र वहतां रथेन।
गृहान् गच्छ गृहपत्नी यथासो वशिनी त्वं विदथमा वदासि।।२६।।

Let Pūṣan lead you hence, taking your hand,
May the Aśvins carry you forth in a chariot,
Go to the house to be the household's mistress
And speak as Lady to your gathered people.

इह प्रियं प्रजया ते समृध्यतामस्मिन् गृहे गार्हपत्याय जागृहि।
एना पत्या तन्वं१ सं सृजस्वाधा जिव्री विदथमा वदाथः।।२७।।

Be happy, and prosper with your children here,
Be vigilant to rule your household in this home.
Mingle with your husband, then shall you,
In advanced age, address your children.

नीललोहितं भवति कृत्यासक्तिर्व्यज्यते।
एधन्ते अस्या ज्ञातयः पतिर्बन्धेषु बध्यते।।२८।।

Her hue is blue and red,
The fiend who clings close is driven away.
Well thrives the bride's friend,
The husband is bound fast in bonds.

परा देहि शामुल्यं ब्रह्मभ्यो वि भजा वसु।
कृत्यैषा पद्वती भूत्व्या जाया विशते पतिम्।।२९।।

Give away your woollen robe,
Give treasure to the brāhmaṇa priests.
This female fiend has got her feet,
And enters the husband (as) a wife.

अश्रीरा तनूर्भवति रुशती पापयामुया।
पतिर्यद्वध्वो३ वाससा स्वमङ्गमभिधित्सते।।३०।।

Unlovely becomes his body
When it glistens with this wicked fiend,
When time the husband wraps about his limbs
With the bride's garment.

ये वध्वश्चन्द्रं वहतुं यक्ष्मा यन्ति जनादनु।
पुनस्तान् यज्ञिया देवा नयन्तु यत आगताः।।३१।।

Consumptions, from her parents,
Which follow the bride's brilliant chariot,

Let the worshipful gods conduct those back,
from where they came.

मा विदन् परिपन्थिनो य आसीदन्ति दम्पती।
सुगेभिर्दुर्गमतीतामप द्रान्त्वरातयः।।३२।।

Let not the highway thieves pursue the couple,
By pleasant ways let them escape the danger,
And let foes run away.

सुमङ्गलीरियं वधूरिमां समेत पश्यत।
सौभाग्यमस्यै दत्त्वायाथास्तं वि परेतन।।३३।।

Of auspicious omen is this bride,
Come together and see her.
Wishing her good fortune,
Return unto your homes.

तृष्टमेतत्कटुकमेतदपाष्ठवद्विषवन्नैतदत्तवे।
सूर्यां यो ब्रह्मा विद्यात्स इद्वाधूयमर्हति।।३४।।

Pungent is this, and bitter this
Filled, as it were, with arrowbarbs,
Poisoned and not offerable.
The priest who knows Sūryā well
Deserves the garment of the bride.

आशसनं विशसनमथो अधिविकर्तनम्।
सूर्यायाः पश्य रूपाणि तानि ब्रह्मा तु शुन्धति।।३५।।

Carving on, carving open,
also cutting over apart,
Behold the forms of Sūryā,
These does the priest purify.

गृभ्णामि त सौभगत्वाय हस्तं मया पत्या जरदष्टिर्यथासः।
भगो अर्यमा सविता पुरन्धिर्मह्यं त्वादुर्गार्हपत्याय देवाः।।३६।।

I take your hand in mine for good fortune
That you may reach old age with me,
Your husband.
The gods Bhaga, Aryaman, Savitar, Purandhi,
Have given you to be my home's mistress.

तां पूषञ्छिवतमामेरयस्व यस्यां बीजं मनुष्या३ वपन्ति।
या न ऊरू उशती विश्रयाते यस्यामुशन्तः प्रहराम शेपम्।।३७।।

O Pūṣan! send her on as most auspicious,
Her who shall be the sharer of my pleasures;
Her who shall twine her loving arms about me,
And welcome all my love and mine embraces.

तुभ्यमग्रे पर्यवहन्त्सूर्यां वहतुना सह।
पुनः पतिभ्यो जायां दा अग्ने प्रजया सह।।३८।।

For you, in the beginning,
They escorted Sūryā to her home with bridal chariot.
O Agni! Give to us the husband in return,
the wife together with progeny.

पुनः पत्नीमग्निरदादायुषा सह वर्चसा।
दीर्घायुरस्या यः पतिर्जीवाति शरदः शतम्।।३९।।

Agni has given back thc bride,
With splendour and with ample life.
May he who is her husband,
Live a hundred autumns.

सोमः प्रथमो विविदे गन्धर्वो विविद उत्तरः।
तृतीयो अग्निष्टे पतिस्तुरीयस्ते मनुष्यजाः।।४०।।

Soma obtained her first of all,
Next the Gandharva was her lord,

Agni was your third husband,
The fourth, one of human birth.

सोमो ददद् गन्धर्वाय गन्धर्वो ददद‍ग्नये।
रयिं च पुत्राँश्चादादग्निर्मह्यमथो इमाम्।।४१।।

Soma to the Gandharva,
And to Agni the Gandharva gave:
And Agni has given both wealth and progeny
And this my spouse.

इहैव स्तं मा वि यौष्टं विश्वमायुर्व्यश्नुतम्।
क्रीळन्तौ पुत्रैर्नप्तृभिर्मोदमानौ स्वे गृहे।।४२।।

Be you not parted, dwell you here,
Attain full lifetime,
Sporting with sons and grandsons,
Rejoicing in your own abode.

आ नः प्रजां जनयतु प्रजापतिराजरसाय समनक्त्वर्यमा।
अदुर्मङ्गलीः पतिलोकमा विश शं नो भव द्विपदे शं चतुष्पदे।।४३।।

May Prajāpati bless us with progeny,
May Aryamā adorn us until old age come close.
May not inauspicious enter you,
Your husband's house,
bring blessings to our bipeds and our quadrupeds.

अधोरचक्षुरपतिघ्न्येधि शिवा पशुभ्यः सुमनाः सुवर्चाः।
वीरसूर्देवकामा स्योना शं नो भव द्विपदे शं चतुष्पदे।।४४।।

Not terrible-eyed, not husband-slaying,
Pleasant and helpful, very propitious,
of easy control for the home, hero-bearing,
with favouring mind, radiant, gentle-hearted,

Worshipful to the gods,
Bring blessing to our quadrupeds and bipeds.

इमां त्वामिन्द्र मीढ्वः सुपुत्रां सुभगां कृणु।
दशास्यां पुत्राना धेहि पतिमेकादशं कृधि॥४५॥

O Bounteous Indra!
Bless this bride with husband and progeny,
Bless her with ten children,
And the husband's being the eleventh.

सम्राज्ञी श्वशुरे भव सम्राज्ञी श्वश्र्वां भव।
ननान्दरि सम्राज्ञी भव सम्राज्ञी अधि देवृषु॥४६॥

May you be supreme over your father-in-law,
Over your mother-in-law,
Over your sister-in-law,
Over his brothers rule supreme.

समञ्जन्तु विश्वे देवाः समापो हृदयानि नौ।
सं मातरिश्वा सं धाता समु देष्ट्री दधातु नौ॥४७॥

May all the gods and the Waters join our hearts,
May Mātariśvan, Dhātar, and Deṣṭrī
Bind us close together.

Part IV
Other Ṛṣikās not Listed in Bṛhaddevatā

23

Śacī Paulomī

Śacī Paulomī is the seer of *Ṛ̥V* X.159 containing six *mantras*. She is the Ṛ̥ṣikā as well as the Devatā of this *sūktam*. Hence, it is considered as an *ātmastuṭi* — addressed to Self, a song of triumph by Śacī over her rival co-wives. Being the daughter of Puloma, she has the title Paulomi (*apatya-vācaka*) or Pulomajā. In many places, Indra has been referred as Śacīpati — husband of Śacī, i.e. *Ṛ̥V* IV.30.17, *Ṛ̥V* I.106.6, *Ṛ̥V* VIII.14.2, etc. Śacī also has been presented as Indrapatnī in *Ṛ̥V* I.30.15, *Ṛ̥V* I.62.12, *Ṛ̥V* III.60.6, *Ṛ̥V* IV.20.9, etc. *Matsya Purāṇa* presents her as the daughter of the demon king Puloma, who was the son of Dakṣaputrī Danu and Kaśyapa. Because of her intense worship to Lord Śiva, she became Indra's consort — the Indrāṇī. Bṛ̥haddevatākāra has described her as — *paulomī svān-guṇāns-tatra sapatnīnāṁ ca śaṁsati.*[1] Ācārya Sāyaṇa has confirmed this in his *Bhāṣyam* — *pulomatanayā śacī svātmānam-anena-astaut, ataḥ saivaṛ̥ṣiḥ saiva devatā.*[2]

Ṛ̥V X.159 (6 mantras)

ऋषिका - शची पौलोमी। देवता - शची (आत्मतुष्टि)।

छन्द - अनुष्टुप्।

Ṛ̥ṣikā — Śacī Paulomī

Devatā — Śacī Paulomī (Self-praise)

Metre — Anuṣṭup

1. *Bṛ̥had.*, VIII.63.
2. *Ṛ̥V.Sā.Bh.*, X.159.

उदसौ सूर्यो अगादुदयं मामको भगः।
अहं तद्विद्वला पतिमभ्यसाक्षि विषासहिः॥१॥

The Sun has mounted up,
And this my happy fate has mounted high.
I knowing this, as conqueror,
Have won my husband for mine own.

अहं केतुरहं मूर्धाहमुग्रा विवाचनी।
ममेदनु क्रतुं पतिः सेहानाया उपाचरेत्॥२॥

I am the banner and the head,
A mighty arbitress am I, victorious I am,
And my Lord shall be submissive to my will.

मम पुत्राः शत्रुहणोऽथो मे दुहिता विराट्।
उताहमस्मि संजया पत्यौ मे श्लोक उत्तमः॥३॥

My Sons are slayers of the foe,
My Daughter is a ruling Queen.
I am victorious, over my Lord,
My song of triumph is supreme.

यनेन्द्रो हविषा कृत्व्यभवद् द्युम्न्युत्तमः।
इदं तदक्रि देवा असपत्ना किलाभुवम्॥४॥

Oblation, that which Indra gave,
And thus grew glorious and most high,
This have I offered, O you Gods,
And rid me of each rival wife.

असपत्ना सपत्नघ्नी जयन्त्यभिभूवरी।
आवृक्षमन्यासां वर्चो राधो अस्थेयसामिव॥५॥

Destroyer of the rival wife,
Sole Spouse, victorious, conqueror,

The others' glory have I seized as 'twere
The wealth of weaker dames.

समजैषमिमा अहं सपत्नीरभिभूवरी।
यथाहमस्य वीरस्य विराजानि जनस्य च।।६।।

I have subdued as conqueror these rivals,
These my co-wives,
That I may hold imperial sway over this Hero,
And the folk.

24

Śikhaṇḍinī Kāśyapī

Śikhaṇḍinī Kāśyapī are the two daughters, celestial nymphs, of Ṛṣi Kaśyapa, one of the *saptarṣis*. *ṚV* IX.104 addressed to Pavamāna Soma containing six *mantras*, is alternatively attributed to these celestial sisters. Incidentally, Ṛṣi Kaśyapa's son Bhūtāṁśa is also a Ṛgvedic Seer (*ṚV* X.106). Ācārya Sāyaṇa has described these two sisters as celestial nymphs — *kāṇau parvata-naradāvṛṣi. athavā kaśapasya putryau śikhaṇḍinyākhye dve apsarasāvasya sūktasya draṣṭryau.*[1]

ṚV IX.104 (6 mantras)

ऋषि – पर्वत काण्व, नारद काण्व,
शिखण्डिन्यावप्सरसौ काश्यप्यौ (ऋषिका) वा।
देवता – पवमानः सोमः। छन्द – उष्णिक्।

Ṛṣi — Parvata Kāṇva and Nārada Kāṇva,
or Śikhaṇḍinī Kāśyapī (Ṛṣikās)
Devatā — Pavamāna Soma; Metre — Uṣṇik

सखाय आ नि षीदत पुनानाय प्र गायत।
शिशुं न यज्ञैः परि भूषत श्रिये॥१॥

Sit down, O friends, and sing aloud to him,
Who purifies himself,
Deck him for glory, like a child, with holy rites.

समीं वत्सं न मातृभिः सृजता गयसाधनम्।
देवाव्यं१ मदमभि द्विशवसम्॥२॥

1. *ṚV.Sā.Bh.*, IX.104.

Unite him bringing household wealth,
Even as a calf, with mother kine.
Him who has double strength,
The God-delighting juice.

पुनाता दक्षसाधनं यथा शर्धाय वीतये।
यथा मित्राय वरुणाय शंतमः।।३।।

Purify him who gives us power,
That he, most Blessed One, may be,
A banquet for the Troop, Mitra, and Varuṇa.

अस्मभ्यं त्वा वसुविदमभि वाणीरनूषत।
गोभिष्टे वर्णमभि वासयामसि।।४।।

Voices have sung aloud to you,
As discoverer of wealth for us,
We clothe the hue you wear,
With a robe of milk.

स नो मदानां पत इन्दो देवप्सरा असि।
सखेव सख्ये गातुवित्तमो भव।।५।।

You, Indu, are the food of Gods,
O Sovereign of all gladdening drinks,
As Friend for friend,
Be you best finder of success.

सनेमि कृध्य१स्मदा रक्षसं कं चिदत्रिणम्।
अपादेवं द्वयुमंहो युयोधि नः।।६।।

Drive utterly away from us each demon,
Each voracious fiend, The godless and the false,
Keep sorrow far away.

25

Indrasnuṣā-Vasukrapatnī

INDRASNUṢĀ-VASUKRAPATNĪ is the daughter-in-law of Indra, and wife of Vasukra, son of Indra. *R̥V* X.28 containing 12 *mantras*, is a conversation between Indrasnuṣā, Vasukra and Indra. The first *mantra* is spoken by Indrasnuṣā invoking Indra, in ignorance, says the legend, since her father-in-law is present in disguise. The *sūkta* is a dialogue between father Indra and son Vasukra Aindra. Ācārya Sāyaṇa has described thus — *taṁ vasukrapatnīndrāgamanākāṅkṣiṇī viprakr̥ṣṭam-ivādyayāstaut, atas-tasyāḥ sarṣiḥ, indro devatā.*[1] Br̥haddevatākāra has referred to this *snuṣendrasyāgatān-devan dr̥sṭvā śakramanāgatam. . . .*[2]

R̥V X.28 (12 mantras)

ऋषि – १ इन्द्रस्नुषा वसुक्रपत्नी (ऋषिका);

२, ६, ८, १०, १२ इन्द्रः ३-५, ७, ९, ११ वसुक्र ऐन्द्रः।

देवता – २, ६, ८, १०,१२ वसुक्र ऐन्द्रः,

१, ३-५, ७, ९, ११ इन्द्रः छन्द – त्रिष्टुप्।

R̥ṣis — 1 Indrasnuṣā-Vasukrapatnī (R̥ṣikā),

2, 6, 8, 10, 12 Indra, 3-5, 7, 9, 11 Vasukra Aindra

Devatā — 2, 6, 8, 10, 12 Vasukra Aindra, 1, 3-5, 7, 9, 11 Indra

Metre — Triṣṭup

विश्वो ह्य१न्यो अरिराजगाम ममेदह श्वशुरो ना जगाम।
जक्षीयाद्धाना उत सोम पपीयात्स्वाशितः पुनरस्तं जगायात्।।१।।

---

1. *R̥V.Sā Bh.*, X.28.
2. *Br̥had.*, VII.30.

Now all my other friends are here assembled,
my Father-in-law alone has not come here,
So might he eat the grain and drink the Soma,
And, satisfied, return unto his dwelling.

स रोरुवद् वृषभस्तिग्मशृङ्गो वर्ष्मन्तस्थौ वरिमन्ना पृथिव्याः।
विश्वेष्वेनं वृजनेषु पामि यो मे कुक्षी सुतसोमः पृणाति।।२।।

Loud bellows the Bull whose horns are sharpened,
Upon the height above earth's breadth he stands.
That man I guard and save in all his troubles
Who fills my flanks when he has shed the Soma.

अद्रिणा ते मन्दिन इन्द्र तूयान्त्सुन्वन्ति सोमान्पिबसि त्वमेषाम्।
पचन्ति ते वृषभाँ अत्सि तेषाँ पृक्षेण यन्मघवन्हूयमानः।।३।।

Men with the stone press out for you, O Indra!
Strong, gladdening Soma, and thereof you drink.
Bulls they dress for you, and of these you eat,
When Maghavan, with food you are invited.

इदं सु मे जरितरा चिकिद्धि प्रतीपं शापं नद्यो वहन्ति।
लोपाशः सिंहं प्रत्यञ्चमत्साः क्रोष्टा वराहं निरतक्त कक्षात्।।४।।

Resolve for me, O singer! This my riddle,
The rivers send their swelling water backward,
The fox steals up to the approaching lion,
The jackal drives the wild boar from the brushwood.

कथा त एतदहमा चिकेतं गृत्सस्य पाकस्तवसो मनीषाम्।
त्वं नो विद्वाँ ऋतुथा वि वोचो यमर्धं ते मघवन् क्षेम्याः धूः।।५।।

How shall I solve this riddle, I, the simple,
Declare the thought of you, the Wise and Mighty?
Tell us, well knowing, as befits the season,
Where is your prosperous car advancing?

एवा हि मां तवसं वर्धयन्ति दिवश्चिन्मे बृहत उत्तरा धूः।
पुरू सहस्रा नि शिशामि साकमशत्रुं हि मा जनीता जजान।।६।।

Thus do they magnify me, me the mighty,
Higher than even high heaven is my car-pole.
I, all at once demolish many thousands,
My Father begot me with no foe to match me.

एवा हि मां तवसं जज्ञुरुग्रं कर्मन्कर्मन्वृषणमिन्द्र देवाः।
वधीं वृत्रं वज्रेण मन्दसानोऽप व्रजं महिना दाशुषे वम्।।७।।

Yes, and the Gods have known me also, Indra!
As mighty, fierce and strong in every exploit.
Jubilant with the bolt, I slaughtered Vṛtra,
And for the offerer opened with might the cow-stall.

देवास आयन्परशूँरबिभ्रन् वना वृश्चन्तो अभि विड्भिरायन्।
नि सुद्रवं१ दधतो वक्षणासु यत्रा कृपीटमनु तद्दहन्ति।।८।।

The Deities approached, they carried axes,
Splitting the wood, they came with their attendants.
They laid good timber in the fire-receivers,
And burnt the grass up where they found it growing.

शशः क्षुरं प्रत्यञ्चं जगाराद्रिं लोगेन व्यभेदमारात्।
बृहन्तं चिदृहते रन्धयानि पयद्वत्सो वृषभं शूशुवानः।।९।।

The hare has swallowed up the opposing razor,
I split apart with a clod the distant mountain.
The great will I make subject to the little,
the calf shall wax in strength, and eat the bullock.

सुपर्ण इत्था नखमा सिषायावरुद्धः परिपदं न सिंहः।
निरुद्धश्चिन्महिषस्तर्ष्यावान् गोधा तस्मा अयथं कर्षदेतत्।।१०।।

There has the strong-winged eagle left his claws,
As a snared lion leaves the trap that caught him.

Even the wild steer in his thirst is captured,
The leather strap still holds his foot entangled.

तेभ्यो गोधा अयथं कर्षदेतद्ये ब्रह्मणः प्रतिपीयन्त्यन्नैः।
सिम उक्ष्णोऽवसृष्टाँ अदन्ति स्वयं बलानि तन्वः शृणानाः॥११॥

So may the leather strap their foot entangle
Who fatten on the food of the Brahman.
They all devour the bulls set free to wander,
While they themselves destroy their bodies vigour.

एते शमीभिः सुशमी अभूवन् ये हिन्विरे तन्व१ः सोम उक्थैः।
नृवद्वदन्नुप नो माहि वाजान् दिवि श्रवो दधिषे नाम वीरः॥१२॥

They were well occupied with holy duties,
Who sped in person with their lauds to Soma.
Speaking like man, give us wealth and booty:
In heaven you have the name and fame of Hero.

Appendix A

Ṛṣikās of the Yajurveda

Lopāmudrā — A Ṛgvedic seer (*ṚV* I.179.1-2) is also the seer of *Yajurveda-kaṇḍikās* XVII.11-15 (11, 12, 15 addressed to Agni and 13, 14 addressed to the Prāṇas), and XXXVI.20 addressed to Agni. *Sarvānukramaṇī* presents her as —*namaste bṛhatīm-āgneyīm-ṛṣisutā lopāmudrā.*[1] Ācārya Mahīdhara has clarified further his *Śukla-Yajurveda-Bhāṣyam* — *āgneyī bṛhatī lopāmudrā dṛṣṭā.*[2] She is named Ṛṣi-sutā Lopāmudrā in *Yajurveda.*

Saraśvatī — Along with Prajāpati and the Aśvin-Kumārs, is the seer of *YV* XIX.1 addressed to Soma and Sūrya, and *YV* XXVIII.1-22 and 24-45 addressed to various deities. *Sarvānukramaṇī* confirms her seerhood — *atha sautrāmaṇī-prajāpaterārṣam-aśvinoḥ sarasvatyāśca svādvīṁ tvānuṣṭup. . . .*[3] Ācārya Mahīdhara has presented her in his *Yajurveda-Bhāṣyam* — *sautrāmaṇī-mantrāṇāṁ prajāpatyaśvin-sarasvatya ṛṣayaḥ.*[4]

Kaśipā Bharadvāja-duhitā — A Ṛgvedic (*ṚV* X.127) Ṛṣikā is also the seer of *YV* XXXIV-32. This single *mantra* is addressed to Rātri. Maharṣi Kātyāyana describes her in his *Sarvānukramaṇī* as — *ā rātri pārthiva-bṛhatīṁ rātridevatyāṁ kaśipā bharadvāja-duhitā.*[5]

---

1. *Sar.*, II.24.
2. *YV.Ma.Bh.* XVI.11
3. *Sar.*, II.33.
4. *YV.Ma.Bh.*, XIX.1.
5. *Sar.*, IV.2.

Viśvavārā Ātreyī — Not exactly a Yajurvedic Ṛṣikā. One of her *mantras* *ṚV* V.28.3 is repeated in *YV* XXXIII.12 crediting her. She is named Atri-duhitā Viśvavārā in *Yajurveda.*

Sārparājñī — Not exactly a Yajurvedic Ṛṣikā. She is a Ṛgvedic Ṛṣikā of *ṚV* X.189 addressed to Sārparājñī (herself) or Sūryā containing three *mantras*. Interestingly, these three *mantras* have been repeated in the other three Vedas, i.e. *Yajurveda* III.6-8 (addressed to Agni), *Sāmaveda* 630-632 (addressed to Sūryā or Ātmā), 1376-1378 (addressed to Sūryā or Ātmā) and *Atharvaveda* VI.31.1-3 (addressed to Gau, and credited to Uparivrabhava) XX.48.4-6 (addressed to Gau, Sūryā). Mahīdhara describes her as — *āyaṁ-gaurityādīnāṁ tisṛṇāṁ ṛcāṁ sārparājñīti nāmadheyam.*[6]

6. *ŚYV.Ma.Bh.,* III.6.

Appendix B

Ṛṣikās of the Sāmaveda

Godhā — Again not exactly a Sāmavedic Ṛṣikā. Of the one-and-half *mantras* seen in *Ṛgveda* by her, *ṚV* X.134.7 is repeated with minor changes as *YV* VII.176 and is credited to her. Both are addressed to Indra.

Indramātaraḥ — Again not exactly a Sāmavedic Ṛṣikā. Indramātaraḥ (mothers of Indra)/Deva-bhaginī-samūha are the seers of *ṚV* X.153 addressed to Indra, comprising five *mantras*. Two *mantras* of this *sūkta* with minor modifications are available in the *Sāmaveda* (*ṚV* X.153.2 = *SV* 120) and (*ṚV* X.153.2 = *SV* 175), that are also credited to Indramātaraḥ.

Sārparājñī — Not exactly a Sāmavedic Ṛṣikā. As clarified before, she is a Ṛgvedic Ṛṣikā of *ṚV* X.189 addressed to Sārparājñī (herself) or Sūryā, containing three *mantras*. These three *mantras* have been repeated in the other three Vedas — *Yajurveda* III.6-8 (addressed to Agni), *Sāmaveda* 630-632 (addressed to Sūryā or Ātmā), 1376-1378 (addressed to Sūryā or Ātmā) and *Atharvaveda* VI.31.1-3 (addressed to Gau, and credited to Uparivrabhava) XX.48.4-6 (addressed to Gau, Sūryā).

Appendix C

Ṛṣikās of the Atharvaveda

Indrāṇī — is originally a Ṛgvedic Ṛṣikā. Her *ṚV* X.86 Indra-Indrāṇī-Vṛṣākapi trialogue is repeated *in toto* as *AV* XX.119.

Indramātaraḥ — Is/are the seer of *AV* XX.93. Of the eight *mantra*s that this contains, five *mantra*s *AV* XX.93.4-8 are repetitions of *ṚV* X.153. In *Atharvaveda* she/they is/are known as Devajāmi.

Sūryā-Sāvitrī — Two complete *kāṇḍa*s of *Atharvaveda,* i.e. *AV* XIV.1 (containing 64 *mantra*s) and 2 (containing 75 *mantra*s) are Wedding-Hymns, and are attributed to Sūryā-Sāvitrī. Of the 47 *mantra*s of *ṚV* X.85 titled Vivāha-Sūktam, at least 42 are repeated *in toto*, or with some changes, and in different sequence in the fourteenth (31 *mantra*s repeated) and fifteenth (11 *mantra*s repeated) *kāṇḍa*s of *Atharvaveda* credited to Sūryā-Sāvitrī. Both the *kāṇḍa*s are about her/Vedic wedding, the seer also being Sūryā-Sāvitrī.

Sārparājñī — Not exactly an Atharvavedic Ṛṣikā. As clarified before, she is a Ṛgvedic Ṛṣikā of *ṚV* X.189, addressed to Sārparājñī (herself) or Sūryā containing three *mantra*s. These three *mantra*s have been repeated in the other three Vedas, i.e. *Yajurveda* III.6-8 (addressed to Agni), *Sāmaveda* 630-632 and *Sāmaveda* 1376-1378 (both addressed to Sūryā or Ātmā) and *Atharvaveda* VI.31.1-3 (addressed to Gau, and credited to Uparivrabhava), and *Atharvaveda* XX.48.4-6 (addressed to Gau, Sūryā), however are credited to her.

Appendix D

Gārgī Vācaknavī

Gārgī Vācaknavī was the daughter of Ṛṣi Vacaknu and was a *Brahmavādinī*. She had composed several hymns that questioned the origin of all existence. When King Janaka of Videha organised a *brahmayajña*, a philosophic congress centred on the fire sacrament, Gārgī was one of the eminent participants. She challenged Sage Yājñavalkya with a volley of perturbing questions on Ātmā that confounded Yājñavalkya who had until then silenced many an eminent scholar. Her question — "The layer that is above sky and below earth, which is described as being situated between the earth and the sky, and which is indicated as the symbol of the past, present and future, where is that situated?" confounded even the great Vedic men of letters. She challenged Yājñavalkya twice in debates in King Janaka's court, as documented in the sixth and eighth Brāhmaṇa of the third chapter of *Bṛhadāraṇyaka Upaniṣad*.

Yoga-Yājñavalkya-Saṁhitā, a classical treatise on Yoga attributed to Yājñavalkya is a dialogue between him and Gārgī. Technically, although Gārgī Vācaknvī was a *brahmavādinī*, she was not a Ṛṣikā, i.e. a *mantradraṣṭā*.

Appendix E

Maitreyī

Maitreyī also was not a Ṛṣikā as is innocently believed. She was an *uttama adhikārī* for receiving *brahma-vidyā*. She was the niece of Gārgī, and married Yājñavalkya only to receive the *brahma-vidyā*, as the story goes. One day Yājñavalkya decides to become a Sannyāsī and wanted to distribute his wealth between Kātyāyanī and Maitreyī. Maitreyī asks him whether all the wealth in the world will make her immortal. Yājñavalkya replies *na vittena āśā asti*. She then asks for the wealth of immortality. Yājñavalkya teaches her *brahma-vidyā* which is fourth Brāhmaṇa of second chapter of *Bṛhadāraṇyaka Upaniṣad*.

Conclusion

Beauty of a flower lies more in its fragrance than in its looks and colour. So, to ascertain the fragrance you need to smell it. This is the case with the Vedas and Upaniṣaḍs. The Vedas have never and nowhere forsaken women from delving deep into the *brahma-vidyā* and thereby enhance their social standing or spiritual status. But denying women access to these scriptures in the post-Vedic period has, of course, deprived them for too long of the Vedas. It thus depraved them of their societal right of equality and justice that they had been enjoying in the Vedic period. The factual statements made in this book, based on the Vedic hymns, are indicative enough that *brahma-vidyā* was not an exclusive domain of the menfolk, but was available to all, irrespective of gender, without any prejudice. If there were R̥ṣis in abundance, there was no dearth of R̥ṣikās in *R̥gveda Saṁhitā*. The women of India, as well as the whole world must therefore take great pride in knowing their glorious past, and challenge any obstacles that surface in the path of learning the Vedas or/and the Upaniṣads.

The earliest of the four Vedas, i.e. *R̥gveda* has original *mantras*. *Kr̥ṣṇa-Yajurveda* has 700 hymns from *R̥gveda Saṁhitā*. 20 per cent of *Atharvaveda* are from *R̥gveda* with variations in readings. Of the 1,875 *sāmans* of *Sāmaveda Raṇāyanīya-Śākhā*, 1,504 are from *R̥gveda*.

Indrāṇi's Sapatnībādhana Upaniṣat and Śacī Paulomi's

Ātmastuti are in the same spirit; to subdue the rival co-wives and obtain the affection of her all powerful consort Indra. Ghoṣā is desirous of a married life, and prays to the Aśvins; Apālā is married but deserted, and seeks to be reunited with her estranged husband. Śaśvati Āṅgirasī, on the other hand, is happy to get back her husband. Lopāmudrā, with deep longing for love, seeks conjugal bliss. Śraddhā and Dakṣiṇā complement each other. Śraddhā Kāmāyanī extols the attitude of *śraddhā*, and Dakṣiṇā Prājāpatyā praises charitable donors. Vāgāṁbhṛṇī's Devī-Sūktam is the one I personally admire the most, since it is the free expression of her enlightenment, which can be convincingly compared to Vāmadeva's *ahaṁ manurabhavam, sūryaścāham* in *ṚV* IV.26.1, or Triśaṅku's *ahaṁ vṛkṣasya rerivā* in *Taittirīya Upaniṣad* I.10.

The details of Sūryā-Sāvitrī-Sūktam or the Wedding Hymns are vividly descriptive, very beautiful, and quite touching. The additional *mantras* in the *Atharvaveda* are an admirable supplement. All these narrations, hymns and *mantras* are indicative that the Vedic society desired to live and consequantly lived a happy and complete life with celebration on this planet and did not want to blow it up in search or temptations of the afterlife, which became the theme of the Upaniṣads.

No.	Ṛṣikās	Sūktas
	Who praised the Deities	
1	Ghoṣā Kākṣīvatī, a princess, daughter of Kakṣivān	X.39 (14 *mantras*) X.40 (14 *mantras*)
2	Godhā	X.134.7 (1 *mantra*)+ +SV (1½ *mantra*)
3	Viśvavārā Ātreyī	V.28 (6 *mantras*)
4	Apālā Ātreyī (daughter of Atri)	VIII.91 (7 *mantras*)
5	Juhū-Brahmajāyā (wife of Bṛhaspati)	X.109 (7 *mantras*)

6	Agastya-svasā (sister of Agastya)	X.60.6 (1 *mantra*)
7	Aditi or Aditi-Dākṣyāyanī	IV.18.2nd half of 4 & 7 (2½ *mantras*) and X.72 (9 *mantras*)
	Who Conversed with the Seers and Deities	
8	Indrāṇī (consort of Indra)	X.86. (12 *mantras*), X.145 (6 *mantras*) (*sapatnī-bādhana*)
9	*Indramātaraḥ* (mothers of Indra)	X.153 (5 *mantras*)
10	Saramā Devaśunī (Ṛṣikā)	X.108 (6 *mantras*) (Saramā-Paṇi-Saṁvāda)
11	Romaśā (daughter of Bṛhaspati and wife of King Svanaya Bhāvayava)	I.126.7 (1 *mantra*)
12	Urvaśī (a celestial nymph)	X.95 (9 *mantras*) (Purūravā-Urvaśī-Saṁvāda)
13	Lopāmudrā (wife of Agastya)	I.179.1 & 2 (2 *mantras*)
14	Nadyaḥ (the Rivers)	III.33 (4 *mantras*)
15	Yamī Vaivasvatī (sister of Yama)	X.10 (8 *mantras* – Yama-Yamī Saṁvāda), X.154 (5 *mantras*)
16	Śaśvatī Āṅgirasī (daughter of Aṅgiras, wife of Asaṅga)	VIII.1.34 (1 *mantra*)
	Who Praised the Self (Ātmastuti)	
17	Sārparājñī	X.189 (3 *mantras*)
18	Vāgāmbhṛṇī	X.125 (8 *mantras*) (Devī Sūktam)
19	Śraddhā Kāmāyanī	X.151 (5 *mantras*) (Śraddhā-Sūktam)
20	Dakṣiṇā Prājāpatyā	X.107 (11 *mantras*)
21	Rātri-Bhāradvājī	X.127 (8 *mantras*) (Rātri-Sūktam also chanted in *Durgāsapataśatī Caṇḍi*)

22	Sūryā-Sāvitrī (daughter of Sūrya)	X.85 (47 *mantras*) (used in Wedding)
Other Ṛṣikās not Listed in *Bṛhaddevatā*		
23	Śacī Paulomī	X.159 (6 *mantras*) (Ātmatuṣṭi — addressed to Self)
24	Śikhaṇḍinī Kāśyapī (two daughters — celestial nymphs — of Kaśyapa)	IX.104 (6 *mantras*)
25	Vasukrapatnī/Indrasnuṣā (wife of Vasukra, daughter-in-law of Indra)	X.28.1 (1 *mantra*)

Glossary

***Abhicāra*:** Spell, magic, exorcising. Most of the *mantras* in the *Atharvaveda* are spells. *R̥V* X.145 popularly known as Sapatnībādhana Upaniṣat by Indrāṇi is a spell.

Agastya Maitrāvaruṇi: A seer — R̥ṣi, whose *mantras* are available in all the four Vedas. Agastya along with Vasiṣṭha are the sons of Mitra and Varuṇa through Urvaśī, hence the title Maitrāvaruṇi. He is one of the *saptarṣis*. He married Lopāmudrā, who is also a *mantradraṣṭā* — a R̥ṣikā.

Agastya and Vasiṣṭha are the offsprings of Mitra and Varuṇa, whose seed fell from them at the sight of lovely nymph, Urvaśī. Part of the seed fell into a jar and part in water. From the former arose Agastya, who is therefore called *kumbhayoni*, and from the water arose Vasiṣṭha. Cf. *The Student's Sanskrit-English Dictionary*, Vaman Shivram Apte, Delhi: Nag Publishers, 1987, p. 646.

Agni: Agni is a Vedic deity. He is the second most important deity in the Vedas after Indra. More than 200 *sūktas* are dedicated to him. He is a terrestrial Devatā. Agni is considered as the carrier of oblations in subtle form to other deities.

Anuṣṭubh: A kind of metre used in the *R̥gveda* having thirty-two (8 × 4 *pādas*) syllables, with eight syllables per quarter (*pāda*).

Apsaras: Celestial females, given to music and dance. Urvaśī is an *apsarā* (*ṚV* X.95). Other famous *apsaras*es are Menakā (mother of Śakuntalā) and Rambhā.

Aśvins: They are the celestial physicians. More than fifty *sūkta*s are dedicated to them. They are the sons of Vivasvan and Saraṇyū (daughter of Tvaṣṭā).

***Atharvaveda*:** One of the four Vedas after compilation. It (Śaunaka-*śākhā*) is about 56 per cent the size of *Ṛgveda* (Śākala-*śākhā*). Around 20 per cent of its content is repeated from the *Ṛgveda*. It is not used in any Vedic rituals, and comprises spells and charms. Currently, two of its *śākhā*s are extant — Śaunaka and Paippalāda.

***Ākhyāna*:** A story based on legends. Apālā Sūktam is an *ākhyāna*. So is Naciketā in *Kaṭhopaniṣad* (as per *Śāṅkara-Bhāṣyam,* I.1.1).

***Ācārya*:** The title *ācārya* is affixed to the names of learned spiritual leaders. The following *ācārya*s authored commentaries on various texts that are available to us even now, i.e. Śaṅkarācārya (Advaita Vedānta), Rāmānujācārya (Viśiṣṭādvaita), Madhvācārya (Dvaita), Durgācārya (*Nirukta-Bhāṣyam*), Sāyaṇācārya (*Bhāṣyam* on all the four Vedas).

Āprī-sūktam: An Āprī-Sūktam is a particular type of ritual hymn consisting of invocations to a series of deified objects: (i) *idhma* or *samiddha agni,* (ii) *tanūnapāt,* (iii) *nārāśaṁsa,* (iv) *iḷā,* (v) *barhi,* (vi) *divyadvāra,* (vii) *uṣāsānaktā,* (viii) *divyahotā pracetas,* (ix) the three *devī*s — Sarasvatī, Iḷā, Bhāratī, (x) *tvaṣṭā,* (xi) *vanaspati,* (xii) *svāhākṛti,* and said to be introductory to the animal sacrifice. There are ten Āprī-Sūktam in the *Ṛgveda*.

***Ārṣa*:** A *taddhita*-form derived from the word Ṛṣi. Means Ṛṣi-*prayoga,* meaning any discipline born of a Ṛṣi.

Indra: He is the most important Vedic deity. More than 250 *sūkta*s are dedicated to him. He is a god of the mid-region. He was all powerful, until Lord Kṛṣṇa vanquished him (Govardhanadhārī episode in the *Bhāgavatam*) replacing his worship with the worship of Nature.

Upaniṣad: Knowledge regarding the reality of *Brahman, brahma-vidyā: vedānto nāma-upaniṣat-pramāṇam — Ve.Sā*; the concluding portions of the Vedas. Secret knowledge, mystical knowledge: *ya evaṁ veda, iti-upaniṣat — Ma.Nā.Up*; XXII.2.

Uṣṇik: A kind of metre used in the *Ṛgveda* having twenty-eight (8 + 8 + 12) syllables, in three quarters (*pāda*s).

***Ṛgveda*:** The most ancient sacred text of the Hindus consisting of 1,028 *sūkta*s — hymns (including the 11 Bālakhilya hymns) arranged in ten *maṇḍala*s or eight *aṣṭaka*s.

Ṛṣi: *ṛṣati jānāti iti ṛṣiḥ* — one who is a *mantra-draṣṭā* — seer or composer of Vedic hymns. It also denotes the person/or being who sees the *mantra*(s) as the definition — *yasya vākyaṁ sa ṛṣi, yā tenocyate sā devatā*. Thus *nadyaḥ* (the rivers) and Saramā (the celestial female dog) are titled Ṛṣis in the *sūkta*s.

Ṛṣikā: A female Ṛṣi. There are twenty-seven Ṛṣikās in the *Ṛgveda*, listed in the *Bṛhaddevatā* of Śaunaka.

***Kāṇḍa*s:** Books.

***Kaṇḍikā*:** A part of a book. One *kāṇḍa* is divided into many *kaṇḍikā*s as in the *Atharvaveda*.

Kakṣivān Dairghatamas: He is the Ṛṣi for *ṚV* I.116-126. He is the son of Ṛṣi Dīrghatamas (seer of *ṚV* I.140-164) through a maid of the king of Aṅga, named Uśij, who desired a son from him. Being their son, Kakṣivān is known as Kakṣivān Dairghatamas Auśija.

Kātyāyana: Author of *Sarvānukramaṇī*.

Kālidāsa: A renowned poet and dramatist in Sanskrit belonging to first-fourth century CE. His famous plays are

Mālavikāgnimitram, Abhijñānaśākuntalam and *Vikramorvaśīyam*. His epic poems (*mahā-kāvyas*) are *Raghuvaṁśa* and *Kumārasaṁbhavam*. Thus, out of five recognized *mahā-kāvyas* in Sanskrit literature, two were composed by him. He has also composed two *khaṇḍa-kāvyas* — *Ṛtusaṁhāra* and *Meghadūtam*.

***Khila*:** Supplementary hymns.

Gandharvas: Celestial males, given to music and dance.

Gāyatrī: A kind of metre used in the *Ṛgveda* having twenty-four (8 × 3 *pādas*) syllables, arranged in a triplet of eight syllables each.

***Chandas*:** The Vedas. Also means discipline of prosody and metres. One of the six Vedāṅgas — Śīkṣā, Kalpa, Vyākaraṇa, Nirukta, Chandas and Jyotiṣa. There are many metres used in the *Ṛgveda*, list of which is given in *ṚV* X.130.4.

***Chāndogya Upaniṣad*:** It is the most voluminous Upaniṣad and is attached to Talavakāra-śākhā of *Sāmaveda*. It has eight *adhyāyas* (chapters), 152 *khaṇḍas* (sub-chapters) and 600 *mantras*. Chapter six contains Uddālaka Āruṇi teaching *brahma-vidyā* to his son Śvetaketu. Chapter 7 contains Sanatakumāra's teaching *brahma-vidyā* to Sage Nārada. The first five chapters are *upāsanās* (meditations). Teachings of Uddālaka is more cogent than Yājñavalkya's.

Jagatī: A kind of metre used in the *Ṛgveda* having forty-eight syllables.

Triṣṭubh: A kind of metre used in the *Ṛgveda* having forty-four (11 × 4 *pādas*) syllables, with eleven syllables per quarter (*pāda*).

***Dakṣiṇā*:** 1. Priestly gift offered by the *yajamāna* (host) to the brāhmaṇas at the completion of any religious rite. 2. Any offering given as a gift of gratitude by a student, devotee or individual to a teacher, guru or a *mahātmā, sādhu*.

Devatā: Technically means a celestial god like Indra, Agni, Marut and Aśvins etc. in the Vedas. Also means any one, to whom a *mantra/sūktam* is addressed to as per the definition *yasya vākyā sa ṛṣi, yā tenocyate sā devatā*. Thus Nadyaḥ (the rivers) and Saramā (the celestial female dog) are titled Devatā in the *sūkta*s. Yama and Yamī, Purūravā and Urvaśī, Saramā and the Paṇis become Ṛṣi and Devatā to each other in their dialogue-hymns.

***Durgā-Saptaśatī*:** Contains 700 *śloka*s describing the conquest of Devī Durgā in vanquishing and destroying the demons Madhu and Kaiṭabha, Mahiṣāsura, Dhūmralocana, Caṇḍa and Muṇḍa, Raktabīja, Niśumbha, Śumbha and their armies, and in blessing King Suratha and Samādhi, a businessman. It is found in *Mārkaṇḍeya Purāṇa*. It contains Rātri-Sūktam (*ṚV* X.127), Devī-Sūktam (*ṚV* X.125).

Navagraha-Sūktam: It is traditionally chanted in the temples and at Navagraha worship. Composed based on many original *mantra*s in the *Ṛgveda*.

Paṅkti: A kind of metre used in the *Ṛgveda* having forty (8 × 5 *pāda*s) syllables, with eight syllables per each five quarter (*pāda*).

Patnī: Wife. For example, Vaśukra-patnī means wife of Vaśukra, who is also Indra-snuṣā, Vaśukra being Indra's son. The lady must be having a name, which is not mentioned in the *sūktam*.

Purāṇa: Secondary religious literature after Śruti, Smṛti and Itihāsa. They traditionally deal with five topics (i) *sarga* (creation), (ii) *pratisarga* (dissolution), (iii) *vaṁśa* (lineage), (iv) *manvantarāṇi* (epochs), and (v) *vaṁśānucaritam* (the legends of future lineage).

The eighteen major Purāṇas are divided into three categories — (I) Six Vaiṣṇava Purāṇas: (i) *Viṣṇu*, (ii) *Bhāgavata*, (iii) *Padma*, (iv) *Nāradīya*, (v) *Garuḍa*, (vi) *Varāha*; (II) Six Brahma Purāṇas: (i) *Brahma*, (ii) *Brahmavaivartta*, (iii) *Bhaviṣya*, (iv) *Brahmāṇḍa*, (v) *Vāmana*, (vi) *Mārkaṇḍeya*; and (III) Six Śaiva Purāṇas: (i) *Śiva*, (ii) *Matsya*, (iii) *Liṅga*, (iv) *Skanda*, (v) *Agni* and (vi) *Kūrma*.

Additionally, there are eighteen Upa-Purāṇas.

***Bṛhaddevatā*:** Authored by Śaunaka is an index of the "many gods", a much more extensive work than any other *anukramaṇī*s. It contains about 1,200 *ślokas* in *anuṣṭubh*, occasionally interspersed with *triṣṭubh*s. It is divided into eight *adhyāya*s corresponding to the eight *aṣṭaka*s of the *Ṛgveda*. Following the order of the *Ṛgveda*, its main object is to state the deity for each verse. A peculiarity of this work is that it refers to a number of supplementary hymns (*khila*s) which do not form part of the canonical text of the *Ṛgveda*.

***Bṛhadāraṇyaka Upaniṣad*:** It is attached to *Śukla-Yajurveda*. Literally it means a dense forest. It has six *adhyāya*s (chapters), forty-seven *brāhmaṇa*s (sub-chapters) and 438 *mantra*s. It contains the debates of Yājñavalkya with many great scholars and winning over them. Also his dialogue with his wife Maitreyī teaching her *brahma-vidyā*.

Bṛhatī: A kind of metre used in the *Ṛgveda* having thirty-six syllables, with nine syllables per quarter (*pāda*) or (8 + 8 + 12 + 8) syllables.

***Brahmacārī*:** One who takes up all the disciplines prescribed in the scriptures, so that he gets the *brahma-vidyā*. In a simple sense, a student residing with the teacher and studying scripture(s).

***Brahma-vidyā*:** The equation between Brahman and the *jīva*. In modern language, the energy matter equation $e = mc^2$.

Brāhmaṇa Texts: Each of the four Vedas has Brāhmaṇa texts. There are eighteen Brāhmaṇas extant now. ***Ṛgveda***: (i) *Aitareya*, (ii) *Kauṣitaki*; ***Śukla-Yajurveda***: (iii) *Śatapatha*; ***Kṛṣṇa-Yajurveda***: (iv) *Taittirīya*, (v) *Kaṭha*, (vi) *Maitrāyaṇī*, (vii) *Satyāyaṇī*, (viii) *Bhallaka*; ***Sāmaveda***: (ix) *Jaiminīya*, (x) *Ārṣeya*, (xi) *Tāṇḍya*, (xii) *Ṣaḍviṁśa*, (xiii) *Chāndogya*, (xiv) *Sāmavidhāna*, (xv) *Devatādhyāya*, (xvi) *Saṁhitopaniṣad*, (xvii) *Vaṁśa*; ***Atharvaveda***: (xviii) *Gopatha*.

Manusmṛti: Oft-quoted Dharmaśāstra. Few other famous Dharmaśāstras are — *Āpastamba-Smṛti*, *Gautama-Smṛti*, *Yājñavalkya-Smṛti*, *Vāsiṣṭha-Smṛti*, *Baudhāyana-Smṛti*, *Hārīta-Smṛti* and *Nārada-Smṛti*.

Mātaraḥ: Mothers. For example, Indramātaraḥ (*ṚV* X.153) meaning mothers of Indra.

Yajamāna: The agent for whom the priest(s) perform ritual(s). The chief person in a religious ritual. The *puṇya/apūrva* result of the ritual goes to him as per the scripture. The performing priest(s) receive *dakṣiṇā* for their services rendered.

Yajña: A religious fire ritual.

Yajurveda: One of the four Vedas, where the collection of the *mantras* are in prose-form. *Yajurveda* has two divisions — *Śukla-Yajurveda*, and *Kṛṣṇa-Yajurveda*. Its subject matter is liturgy, fire-rituals and how to perform the same.

Yama: Twin, one of a pair. Also name of the god of death. He is the son of Vivasvat (the Sun) and Saraṇyu, the daughter of Tvaṣṭā. His twin sister is Yamī.

Vāmadeva Gautama: A famous Ṛgvedic Ṛṣi. He is the Ṛṣi of the fourth *maṇḍala* of the seven *vaṁśa-maṇḍala*s in *Ṛgveda*. All the fifty-eight *sūkta*s of *Maṇḍala* IV have been revealed to Vāmadeva and his three descendants, the *vāmadevyaḥ*. The famous declaration *ahaṁ manurabhavaṁ, sūryaścāhaṁ, kakṣivān* *ṛṣiraśmi vipraḥ, ahaṁ kutsaṁ-ārjuneyaṁ nṛyuñjeṣaṁ kaviruśanā paśyatā mā* is in this *maṇḍala.*

Maharṣi Vāmadeva was the son of Ṛṣi Gotama. He is treated as a *gotrakāra*-Ṛṣi.

Vedānta: (lit.) Concluding portions of the Veda. Known as Upaniṣad. Vedāntins consider this as the essence of the Vedas. Name of *darśana* that is directed to the analysis of the Upanìṣads. According to *Ve.Sā.*, "Vedānta is a valid means of knowledge, the *Śārīraka-Sūtra*s and other books that help in the elucidation of its meaning."

Veda: From the root √*vid* — to know, (lit.) knowledge. Collections of scriptures, which were envisioned/channelled by the *ṛsi*s. This vast body of literature has been compiled into four books — *Ṛk, Yajus, Sāma* and *Atharva*. Each of them further divided into four portions or sections — (i) Saṁhitā, (ii) Brāhmaṇa, (iii) Āraṇyaka, and (iv) Upaniṣad. (*Atharvaveda* does not have Āraṇyaka.)

Śatapatha: A group of 100 paths or 100 chapters.

Śatapatha Brāhmaṇa: A Brāhmaṇa text of a group of "hundred paths" or *adhyāya*s (chapters) in *Śukla-Yajurveda*. It is the only Brāhmaṇa connected to *Śukla-Yajurveda*. It is an extensive Brāhmaṇa available in both the *śākhā*s, i.e. Mādhyandina (has 100 *adhyāya*s) and Kāṇva (has 104 *adhyāya*s). In size, this is as big as the *Ṛgveda.*

Śrī Rudram: Śrī Rudram that is chanted in all Śiva temples are *mantra*s from the *Kṛṣṇa-Yajurveda*. In *Śukla-Yajurveda*, chapter XVI is Śrī Rudram.

Saṁvāda-Sūktam: Dialogue-hymns. There are twenty dialogue hymns in the *Ṛgveda*. Some of the famous Saṁvāda-

Sūktas are: Purūravā-Urvaśī-Saṁvāda (*Ṛ̥V* X.95), Yama-Yamī-Saṁvāda (*Ṛ̥V* X.10), Saramā-Paṇi-Saṁvāda (*Ṛ̥V* X.108) and Viśvāmitra-Nadī-Saṁvāda (*Ṛ̥V* III.33).

Few other dialogue-hymns are: Agastya-Lopāmudrā (*Ṛ̥V* I.179), Vaśukrapatnī-Indra-Vaśukra (*Ṛ̥V* X.28), Indrāṇī-Indra-Vṛ̥ṣākapi (*Ṛ̥V* X.86), Vāmadeva-Indra-Aditi (*Ṛ̥V* IV.18), Svanaya Bhāvayavya-Romaśā (*Ṛ̥V* I.126).

Kālidāsa's famous drama *Vikramorvaśīyam* is said to have been based on Purūravā-Urvaśī-Saṁvāda (*Ṛ̥V* X.95).

Sannyāsa: *nyāsa* means renunciation. *Saṁnyāsa* means well-renounced. The fourth stage of life. A person is relieved of his/her social and religious duties so that the person can study the Upaniṣads and obtain *brahma-vidyā* and become free here and now, while living (*jīvan-muktaḥ*).

***Sarvānukramaṇī*:** Authored by Maharṣi Kātyāyana.

***Saptarṣi*:** The seven great Ṛ̥ṣis. The list of *saptarṣi*s differs in the Vedic texts. The earliest list is in *Ja.Br.*, II.218-221 naming — Vasiṣṭha, Bharadvāja, Jamadagni, Gotama, Atri, Viśvāmitra and Agastya. The next list in *Bṛ̥.Up.* II.2.6 has — Gautama, Bharadvāja, Viśvāmitra, Jamadagni, Vasiṣṭha, Kaśyapa and Atri. The *Go.Br.*, I.2.8 lists Vasiṣṭha, Viśvāmitra, Jamadagni, Gautama, Bharadvāja, Guṅgu, Agastya and Kaśyapa.

***Snuṣā*:** Daughter-in-law. Thus, Indra-Snuṣā is Vaśukra-patnī, Vaśukra being Indra's son. The lady must be having a name, which is not mentioned in the *sūktam*.

***Sāmaveda*:** "Veda of Chants", one of the four Vedas. It contains a number of hymns, mostly borrowed from the *Ṛ̥gveda*. Of the 1,875 *sāmans* of *Sāmaveda Rāṇāyanīya-Śākhā*, 1,504 are from *Ṛ̥gveda*. These, set to tune, are chanted by the Sāmavedic priest Udgātā at Soma sacrifices.

Sāyaṇa (before CE 1315-87): The most famous Vedic commentator. Sāyaṇācārya is the only authority, who supposedly commented on all the four Vedas — their Saṁhitās, Brāhmaṇas and few Āraṇyakas. He wrote on many other subjects also.

Sāyaṇa-Bhāṣyam: Supposedly, Sāyaṇa has written commentaries on five Saṁhitās (*Śākala* of *Ṛgveda, Kāṇva* of *Śukla-Yajurveda, Taittirīya* of *Kṛṣṇa-Yajurveda* and *Śaunaka* of *Atharvaveda*), eleven Brāhmaṇas and two Āraṇyakas (*Aitareya* and *Taittirīya*).

"Supposedly", because it is generally accepted that, while Sāyaṇa probably wrote some of the core commentaries attributed to him, which includes contributions of his brother Mādhava, and additions by his students and later commentators who wrote under Sāyaṇa's name. Thus greater parts were written by later commentators, using his name. "Sāyaṇa" (or also Sāyaṇamādhava) by convention refers to the collective authorship of the commentary as a whole without separating such layers. (source-Wikipedia)

***Soma*:** Name of a medicinal plant and its juice used in earliest Vedic sacrifices as offering and inspiration. It is believed to be a rejuvenating drink, definitely not a kind of intoxicant, as people would like to believe. Probably *sarcostema viminalis* or *asclepias acida*.

***Sūkta*:** Literally *su-uktam*, meaning well-said, Ṛgvedic hymn(s). There are 1,028 *sūkta*s in the *Ṛgveda*.

Bibliography

Altekar, A.S., *The Position of Women in Hindu Civilization: From Prehistoric Times to the Present Day*, Delhi: Motilal Banarsidass, 2nd edn. 1959, rpt. 2009.

Aurobindo, Sri, *Hymns to the Mystic Fire*, Pondicherry: Sri Aurobindo Ashram, 1970.

———, Sri, *The Secret of the Veda*, Pondicherry: Sri Aurobindo Ashram, 1st edn. 1956, fifth impression 2005.

Basham, A., *The Wonder That was India*, 3rd rev. edn. 1967, fortieth impression 2003, New Delhi: Rupa & Co.

Chand, Devi (tr.), *The Yajurveda*, 1964. New Delhi: Munshiram Manoharlal, 2004.

Chauhan, D.V., *Understanding Ṛgveda*, 1985, Poona: BORI.

Danino, Michel and Sujata Nahar, *The Invasion That Never Was*, 2nd edn., rev. and enlarged 2001, Delhi: The Mother's Institute of Research, and Mysore: Mira Aditi.

Danino, Michel, *The Lost River: On the Trail of the Sarasvati*, New Delhi: Penguin Books India, 2010.

———, *Indian Culture and India's Future*, New Delhi: D.K. Printworld, first published in India, 2011.

Griffith, Ralph T.H. (tr.), *The Hymns of Ṛgveda*, 2 vols, Delhi: Low Price Publication, 1995.

Schmidt Hanns-Peter, *Some Womenṣ' Rites And Rights*, Poona: BORI, 1987.

Jagannathan, Sakuntala, *Hinduism: An Introduction*, Mumbai: Vakils, Feffer and Simons Pvt. Ltd., 2005.

Kantikar, V.P. and W. Owen Cole, *Hinduism*, London: Hodder Education, 2003.

Kapoor, Kapil and Avadhesh Kumar Singh (eds.), *Indian Knowledge Systems*, vols. 1 and 2, New Delhi: D.K. Printworld, 2005.

Kashyap, R.L. (ed.) *Ṛgveda Mantra Saṁhitā*, Bangalore: Sri Aurobindo Kapali Sastry Institute of Vedic Culture, 2003.

Kashyap, R.L., *In Search of the Ṛgveda, First 121 Sūktas*, Bangalore: Sri Aurobindo Kapali Sastry Institute of Vedic Culture, 2003.

Keith, A.B., *A History of Sanskrit Literature*, Oxford, 1928, Delhi: Motilal Banarsidass, rpt. 1993, 2010.

———, *The Religion and Philosophy of the Vedas and Upanisads.*

Macdonell, A.A., *A History of Sanskrit Literature.* Delhi: Motilal Banarsidass.

———, *A Vedic Grammar for Students*, Delhi: Motilal Banarsidass, 1st Indian edn., 1993, rpt. 2010.

———, *A Vedic Reader for Students*, first published, 1917, Motilal Banarsidass, rpt. 2006.

Max Müller, F., *India: What It Can Teach Us*? Delhi: Vishva Books.

———, *Vedic Hymns*, Sacred Books of the East, vol. 46: rpt., Delhi: Motilal Banarsidass, 2008.

Oldenberg, H. and F. Max Müller, *Vedic Hymns*, 2 vols. Sacred Books of the East. vol. 32, rpt., Delhi: Motilal Banarsidass, 2008.

Pandey, Rajbali, *Hindu Samskaras*, Delhi: Motilal Banarsidass, 2nd rev. edn. 1969, rpt. 1998.

Saraswati, Atmaprajnananda (Swamini), *Nomenclature of the Vedas*, New Delhi: D.K. Printworld, 2012.

Saraswati, Ātmaprajñānanda (Swāmini), *Vision of Vedānta as Reflected in Taittirīyopaniṣad with Special Reference to Śāṅkarabhāṣya*, Ph.D thesis, forthcoming.

Schmidt, Hanns-Peter, *Some Womens' Rites and Rights in the Veda*, Poona: BORI, 1987.

Waterstone, Richard, *India, The Cultural Companion*, London: Duncan Baird Publishers, 2002.

Winternitz, M. and S. Ketkar (tr.), A *History of Indian Literature (1927-33)*, 2 vols., New Delhi: Munshiram Manoharlal, 3rd edn., 1991.

Index

In Devanāgari Sequence

Aśvins, 6-12, 102, 106-07, 110, 134
adhikārī, 3, 132
Aditi/Aditi Dākṣāyanī, 1, 3, 17, 32, 36-37, 135
Agastya Maitrāvaruṇi, 64
Agastya-Lopāmudrā-Saṁvāda, 65
Agastya-svasā, 3, 28, 135
Agni, 19-21, 65, 113-14
Aṅgiras, 78
Anukramaṇikā 28
anuṣṭup, 19, 23, 25, 28, 36, 46, 55, 76, 93, 104, 118
Apālā Ātreyī, 1-3, 22-23, 134
Apālā Sūktam, 22
apsaras, 58
Asamāti King, 28 29
asataḥ sad-ajāyata, 36
asura, 51, 73
Atharvaveda, 49, 88, 102, 128-30, 133-34
ākhyāna, 23
Āprī-Sūktam, 99
Āryans, 67
Ātmastuti, 88, 90, 118, 134
Ātreyī, 19, 22
Indra, 16-17, 22-23, 28, 32, 40-41, 49-52, 79, 115, 123, 129
Indrāṇī, 3, 40-41, 46, 130, 133, 135
Indramātaraḥ, 49, 129, 130, 135
Indrasnuṣā-Vaśukrapatnī, 123, 136
Uṣṇik, 122
Uro Bṛhatī, 104
Urvaśī, 3, 58-59, 104, 135
Ṛgveda, 1-3, 6, 16, 99, 129, 133
Ṛk, 1
Ṛṣi, 1-3
Ṛṣikā, 1-3
Kaśipā Bharadvāja-duhitā, 127
Kakṣivān Dairghatamas, 6, 55
Kālidāsa, 58
Kātyāyana, 19, 127
Kātyāyanī, 132
gandharva(s), 58, 74, 113, 114
Gārgī Vācaknvī, 131, 132
Gāyatrī (a Vedic metre), 19, 28, 49, 88, 100
Gāyatrī-*mantra*, 2
Ghoṣā Kākṣivatī, 1-3, 6-7, 11-15, 134
Godhā, 3, 16, 129, 134
Chāndogya Upaniṣad, 36
Jagatī, 7, 11, 19, 90, 104
Juhū-Brahmajāyā, 3, 25, 134
Taittirīya Upaniṣad, 134

tapas, 2
triṣṭup, 7, 19, 25, 33, 51, 55, 59, 65, 68, 73, 79, 90, 95, 104, 123
Dṛḍhasyu, 64
Dakṣa, 37
Dakṣiṇā Prājāpatyā, 1-2, 4, 95, 134-35
Dīrghatamas, 6
Deva-bhaginī-samūha, 49, 129
devagaṇa, 36
Devajāmi, 49, 130
Devī-Sūktam, 90, 134
draṣṭā, 2
Durgā-Saptaśati, 90, 99
Nadyaḥ/The Rivers, 3, 67, 135
Navagraha-Sūktam, 43, 89
Paṇi, 51
paṅkti, 16, 23, 28, 41, 46
Pavamāna Soma, 122
Purūravā, 58-59
Purūravā-Urvaśī-Saṁvāda, 58-59
Funeral Hymn, 76
Bṛhadāraṇyaka Upaniṣad, 131-32
Bṛhaddevatā, 6, 16, 22, 40, 51, 64, 88, 95
Bṛhaddevatākāra, 3, 19, 25, 32, 40, 49, 55, 58, 64, 78, 90, 93, 99, 102, 118
Bṛhatī, 65, 79
Bhāṣyam, 16, 25, 64, 118
bhāvavṛttam, 4, 76
brahmacārī, 25, 64
Brahmavādinī, 16, 25, 131
Mahābhārata, 58
Mahīdhara, 19, 65, 127-28
Maitreyī, 132
mantra, 1, 3, 16, 19, 22, 25, 28, 32, 40, 49, 51, 58, 67, 72, 78, 88, 90, 93, 95, 102, 121, 123
mantradraṣṭāraḥ, 1, 3, 40, 55
Manusmṛti, 11
Matsya Purāṇa, 118
yajamāna, 95
Yājñavalkya, 131-32
Yajurveda, 19, 65, 88, 127-29
Yama Vaivasvata, 72-73
Yama-Yamī-Saṁvāda, 72-73
Yamī Vaivasvatī, 2-3, 72, 76, 135
Yoga-Yājñavalkya-Saṁhitā, 131
Vāgāmbhṛṇi, 1, 90, 134-35
Vaiśvedeva-Sūktam, 32
Vāk, 3
Vāk-Sūktam, 90
Vāmadeva Gautama, 32-33, 134
Vṛṣākapāyī, 44
Vārṣakapaṁ-Sūktam, 40-41
Vṛsākapi, 40
Vaśukra Aindra, 123
Viśvāmitra Gāthina, 67
Viśvāmitra-Nadī-Saṁvāda, 67
Viśvavārā Ātreyī, 3, 19, 128, 134
Viśvedevā, 25
Vikramorvaśīyam, 58
Vipāṭ, 67
Virāṭsthāna, 73
Vivāha-Sūktam, 102, 104, 130
Vivasvān, 72
Rātri Bhāradvājī, 4, 99-100, 127, 135
Rātri-Sūktam, 99
Romaśā, 3, 55, 57, 135
Lopāmudrā, 3, 64, 127, 134-35

Śaci Paulomi, 2, 118, 133, 136
Śaśvatī Āṅgirasī, 2-3, 78, 134-35
Śatapatha Brāhmaṇa, 58
Śaunaka, 3, 25, 49
Śikhaṇḍinī Kāśyapī, 2, 121, 136
Śraddhā Kāmāyanī, 3, 93, 134-35
Śradhā-Sūktam, 93
Śutudrī, 67
Sāmaveda, 16, 49, 88, 128-29, 133
sannyāsī, 132
sapatnī-bādhana, 40, 46, 133
saptarṣis/sapta ṛṣayaḥ, 23, 25, 64, 121
Saramā Devaśunī, 3, 51, 135
Saramā-Paṇi-Saṁvāda, 51
Sarasvatī, 127
Sārparājñī, 3, 88, 128-30, 135
Sarvānukramaṇī, 19, 127
Savitā, 102
Sāyaṇa, 7, 16, 19, 22, 25, 28, 40, 49, 51, 59, 64, 67, 78, 88, 93, 95, 99, 102, 118, 123
Soma, 113-14
Suhastya Ghauṣeya, 7
sūkta, 2, 6-7, 22, 40, 49, 95, 99, 123
Sūryā-Sāvitrī, 1, 4, 102, 130, 136
Sūryā-Sāvitri-Sūktam, 102, 104, 134
Sūryā-Sūktam, 102, 104
Svanaya Bhāvayavya, 56